SEE YOURSELF
IN CYBER

SEE YOURSELF IN CYBER

Security Careers Beyond Hacking

ED ADAMS

WILEY

To my wife, Maureen, without whom none of this would be possible.

You are not only the light that shines our way to give us clear vision; you are also the rock-solid foundation upon which we stand and build, together, our life. All of my many projects and side projects— you abide, support, enable, and enhance.

Thank you for being so loving, critical, patient, and creative. You challenge me to be better in every way; I am so very blessed and fortunate to have you by my side.

Contents

Contents

The Many Colors of Cybersecurity

Part I of this book explains the many work roles that can, do, should, and might incorporate security as an aspect of the job. I use the analogy of the color wheel to create the *cybersecurity color wheel*, which is split into six segments: the primary colors of red, blue, and yellow, followed by the secondary colors of purple, orange, and green. I also include a chapter solely dedicated to the color white, which sits at the center of the cybersecurity color wheel, touching each of the six color slices.

For the primary colors, I relate many jobs to the Workforce Framework for Cybersecurity (the NICE Framework), as it is one of the few comprehensive efforts that document cybersecurity work roles and the associated knowledge, skills, activities, and tasks associated with each one. However, the NICE Framework is not an accurate depiction of today's cybersecurity workforce. I point out the relevant differences where most appropriate and provide real-world examples of jobs, responsibilities, and career paths in these color slices.

For the secondary colors, the NICE Framework has virtually no coverage when it comes to work roles; however, these colors provide exciting potential for cybersecurity professionals and those interested in integrating security activities into non-security-specific jobs.

The final chapter of Part I is all about the jobs that provide the vision and guardrails for the cybersecurity work done at a given organization. These are the professionals who collect, collate, analyze, and disseminate the security and privacy requirements placed upon the enterprise, translating them into controls for each major workgroup.

Chapter 1

Introduction and Motivation

I am an imposter.

Many people consider me an expert in cybersecurity, particularly software/application security. Yet, I have no degree in cybersecurity. I have zero security industry certifications. I have never been a cybersecurity practitioner for an enterprise or government agency. So I'm a phony, right? A fraud.

Wrong! Like many of us in this industry, I am mostly self-taught. I leveraged the education and experience I had to build the body of knowledge that has become my own—vast and broad and uniquely "Ed." Nobody has the experience and education that I do. I have proven myself time and time again. I am a trusted advisor to my clients, I am a speaker at industry conferences, I am a cybersecurity talk show host, and I am a sought-after expert for that very knowledge and experience only I have. I belong.

Many of us in cybersecurity feel conflicted. We feel as if we don't belong because we haven't "earned our stripes" or we lack some technical degree, certification, or hands-on experience. Imposter syndrome is real. But I'm writing this to let you know that you don't need a technical degree or any particular certification or prior hands-on experience before starting your career in cybersecurity. Cybersecurity has hundreds of different types of jobs, both technical and nontechnical. I have many friends and colleagues in cyber (many holding C-level positions) who graduated with degrees in Spanish, finance, philosophy, and other nontechnical/engineering disciplines. I have undergraduate degrees in mechanical engineering and English literature, as well as a master's in business administration (MBA). Nothing in my education would lead one to think I'd become a cybersecurity "expert"—yet here I am writing this book after spending the past 20 years in the security field. And I love it. You can too.

As executives, hiring managers, HR professionals, and others who create cybersecurity job descriptions and hire practitioners, we need to be mindful that we reflect realistic requirements for job seekers. One of my good friends, who is a CISO, reminds me that she has seen far too many entry-level jobs that require Certified Information Systems Security Professional (CISSP) certification, for example. The CISSP certification requires five years of industry experience before you can even sit for the exam. These paradoxical blockades abound in the cybersecurity industry; it is our obligation and duty to correct them.

How This Book Is Organized

I've organized this book into two parts, covering the following main topics:

- **In Chapters 2–5, we explore cybersecurity careers using the analogy of the color wheel:** I first came across this concept when I saw April Wright deliver a brilliant talk at the 2017 BlackHat USA conference.[1] Other folks, like Louis Cremen in

---

[1] *Orange Is The New Purple*, by April C. Wright For BlackHat USA 2017, www.blackhat.com/docs/us-17/wednesday/us-17-Wright-Orange-Is-The-New-Purple-wp.pdf.

See Yourself in Cyber

2020,[2] expanded on Ms. Wright's talk, and I plan to do the same. I'll discuss cybersecurity via primary colors first (red, blue, and yellow) followed by the blended secondary colors (purple, orange, and green). I also spend time talking about the absence of color in cybersecurity: white jobs. For each of these, I reference what I consider to be the most comprehensive research published on cybersecurity jobs: *The Workforce Framework for Cybersecurity*, commonly referred to as the NICE Framework (see `https://niccs.cisa.gov/workforce-development/nice-framework`), published as part of the National Initiative for Cybersecurity Careers and Studies (NICSS) under the purview of the U.S. Department of Homeland Security's Cybersecurity and Infrastructure Security Agency (CISA). But the NICE Framework is flawed. It doesn't include many common jobs that relate to cybersecurity, and it doesn't address how to incorporate security into noncybersecurity jobs, a crucial necessity for defending our digital enterprises.

- **In Chapter 6, we cover software:** We can't operate today without the enablement of software, so I dedicate a chapter to it and highlight its importance. Regardless of which job you want in cybersecurity, it will be difficult to avoid dealing with software at some level. Most simply it is the fuel for our connected digital world. The vast majority of cybersecurity jobs do not require knowledge of how to code; however, a basic understanding of how software works, as well as how and where it enables technologies such as the Internet of Things (IoT),

---

[2]*Introducing the InfoSec Colour Wheel—Blending Developers with Red and Blue Security Teams*, by Louis Cremen, `https://hackernoon.com/introducing-the-infosec-colour-wheel-blending-evelopers-with-red-and-blue-security-teams-6437c1a07700`.

blockchain, and the cloud is essential. Say you take a job as a cyber audit or risk professional. Without the ability to assess how the software in scope complies with the standards against which you're measuring, you won't be able to do your job effectively.

- **In Chapter 7, we cover diversity and inclusion:** This is a passion of mine. My demographic, middle-aged white males, dominates the cybersecurity workforce in terms of percentage employed. This is a dangerous cybersecurity problem as much as it is a socioeconomic issue. More diverse teams make better decisions, operate more efficiently/profitably, and outperform homogeneous groups; this has been proven in numerous studies. Meanwhile, the cybersecurity industry has millions of unfilled job openings. We have an opportunity to address multiple challenges at once. This is discussed at length in Chapter 7.

- **In Chapter 8, I include interviews and survey results from working cybersecurity practitioners:** One lesson I've learned in my career, sometimes painfully, is that I often need help. Some of the smartest, most successful people I know are quick to point to others who have enabled them, supported them, and otherwise assisted them. I interviewed dozens of cybersecurity professionals and asked them the same set of questions about their origin, what they look for when hiring, and challenges they've faced. I share those insights in this chapter along with data collected from online surveys asking the same questions.

Who This Book Is For

This book has a twofold objective, discussed in the following sections.

For Managers, Directors, Executives, and Other Business Leaders

You'll learn to create a relatable framework for the dozens of cybersecurity jobs that exist. Complement the work done by others, for example, the National Initiative for Cybersecurity Education, with practical experience to help build an understanding of realistic expectations, job descriptions, and recruiting strategies. I also provide insights and views into the many different ways the people in your organization—inhabiting a variety of roles not traditionally associated with cybersecurity—can contribute to improving its cybersecurity backbone. You'll discover how developers, DevOps professionals, managers, and others can strengthen your cybersecurity. You'll also find out how improving your firm's diversity and inclusion can have dramatically positive effects on your team's talent. The book should also be valuable to policymakers, regulators, and compliance professionals who want to better understand the roles, responsibilities, tasks, and contributions various job functions provide to cybersecurity hygiene.

For Individuals Interested in Entering the Industry or Furthering Their Cybersecurity Career

You'll learn to create a similarly relatable framework for cybersecurity jobs, particularly those you might not be aware of. Cybersecurity is popularized by the hackers and defenders. Imagery of black hoodies or massive war rooms with ceiling-high screens showing threat intelligence are commonplace when people imagine cyber. But the reality of the industry can be far more mundane—and far more interesting to those not drawn to hacking and war rooms. If you have a background in finance, legal, psychology, law enforcement, or economics (just as a few examples), you can build a lucrative career in cybersecurity. I also want to paint several pictures for you about the world of cybersecurity that might help broaden your perspective and pique your interest further than where it is now.

About the NICE Framework

The National Institute of Standards and Technology (NIST) developed *The Workforce Framework for Cybersecurity*, also known as the NICE Framework (see https://niccs.cisa.gov/workforce-development/nice-framework). It attempts to be a comprehensive guide to identify and categorize various work roles within the realm of cybersecurity. Its structured approach can help organizations define cybersecurity-related tasks, skills, and competencies required for a successful workforce. It doesn't perfectly reflect job titles that exist in the industry, but I attempt to augment them with actual work roles in each of the color slices covered in this book.

The NICE Framework has three major components:

- Seven categories that provide a high-level grouping of common cybersecurity functions
- Thirty-three specialty areas meant to define distinct areas of cybersecurity work
- Fifty-two work roles, a detailed grouping of cybersecurity jobs comprised of specific *knowledge, skills,* and *abilities* (KSAs) required to perform the work

The work roles and related KSAs are valuable resources for any cybersecurity or human resources leader when contemplating job descriptions, performance evaluation, and career pathing. It is also incredibly useful for job seekers looking to enter or further their career in cybersecurity.

The following are the seven categories of the NICE Framework:

- Securely Provision
- Operate and Maintain
- Oversee and Govern
- Protect and Defend
- Analyze
- Collect and Operate
- Investigate

Some of those phrases don't really jibe with day-to-day job functions. To help, let me translate a couple into more recognizable terms:

- **Securely Provision:** This means build or buy. Think developers (both software and IT system), architects, testers/quality assurance, product managers, procurement teams, and to some extent risk managers (although I could put them in a few of the categories). In the world of DevOps, this is "Dev."

- **Operate and Maintain:** This is your IT system and network operations team. Think system administrators, tech support, and DBAs. In the world of DevOps, this is "Ops."

- **Oversee and Govern:** This is the team that provides leadership and guidance for cybersecurity across all teams. Think C-suite, legal, policy and planning, and, very importantly, security training and awareness.

- **Protect and Defend:** This is the core of day-to-day cybersecurity for many practitioners. It's all about cyber defense, incident response, vulnerability assessment, and management of the

9

security holes identified in the supported IT systems. Here you'll find security operations center (SOC) analysts, penetration testers, security engineers, and many jobs on the information security team.

- **Analyze:** This is a weird one for me because virtually every cybersecurity job function has an analyze component. NICE includes activities such as threat intelligence, exploitation analysis, threat modeling, and even cultural analysis applied to cybersecurity. The work roles NICE lists under this category seldom exist in practice. The most common I see is the threat intelligence analyst (or something of that ilk).

- **Collect and Operate:** This is another oddball. NICE describes this as "specialized denial and deception operations and collection of cybersecurity information that may be used to develop intelligence." I witness this applied in nearly every job function that incorporates security considerations. Devs restrict user input, Ops use firewalls to block certain traffic, Govern defines what can/can't be collected, and so forth. Similar to the Analyze category, I seldom see the work roles NICE list in practice; for example, All Source-Collection Manager (CO-CLO-001) is a job I've never seen listed. Maybe once or twice the term has come across my radar screen as part of a U.S. Department of Defense job posting, but I'm confident it's only in that specific niche and only because of the NICE Framework. Otherwise, the job title simply doesn't exist as part of the cybersecurity industry.

- **Investigate:** This is all about surveillance and forensics. Think cybercrime investigator, digital forensics analyst, special agent (for FBI), and so on. This category is closely related to the world of incident response.

For each of the chapters in which I discuss careers related to a color, I reference the NICE-defined work roles as well as roles I know to exist in practice. Knowing both will help you align your objectives with both an academic/research-based publication as well as the experience of someone with 20 years in the industry who has recruited, hired, and developed hundreds of professionals, either directly or indirectly, related to cybersecurity.

Summary

Now that you've read my motivation for writing this book and understand how it is organized, I hope you will dive in with enthusiasm, ready to learn more about the exciting field of cybersecurity. I have enjoyed the field for the better part of two decades; yet, many remain vexed and confused by cybersecurity jobs and career paths. I have seen far too many cybersecurity leaders, hiring managers, and HR professionals write job descriptions that are fantastical. The result is the disenfranchisement of potential hires who could actually perform very well in the job had it been appropriately described.

We all need to be more mindful to create more realistic requirements for our cyber needs. Cybersecurity leaders can use this book as a reference guide to glean valuable insight into work roles and the associated knowledge, skills, abilities, and tasks for each one related to security. Also, read Chapter 7 on diversity and inclusion with an open mind, as it may provide you with useful tools to cultivate, attract, develop, and retain a more diverse and happy staff. Finally, read how practitioners responded to the interview questions I posed and consume the case studies with an eye toward replicating such success and inspiration in your own organization.

Many individuals keen to learn more about cybersecurity careers don't know where to turn. This book endeavors to provide a plethora of useful information, references, and stories meant to educate, inspire, assist, and hire practitioners. If you are one of these individuals, you can flip through Chapters 2–5, which discuss the cybersecurity color wheel, to learn about jobs related to each color slice. Also, feel free to jump straight to the special subject chapters dedicated to software, diversity, and inclusion, or the advice and case studies.

Chapter 2

The Many Colors of Cybersecurity

In the dynamic realm of cybersecurity, roles and responsibilities span a vast spectrum, encompassing everything from analyzing threats to governing policies and innovating solutions. To better understand this intricate landscape, I draw inspiration from the color wheel, as others before me have. This visual representation of primary and secondary colors blend to create a comprehensive palette of cybersecurity jobs and noncybersecurity jobs alike. For noncybersecurity jobs, I discuss the security aspects of those jobs and how very important they are to executing quality work for that particular function.

As discussed in the previous chapter, *The Workforce Framework for Cybersecurity*, also known as the NICE Framework, serves as a comprehensive guide for identifying and categorizing various work roles within the realm of cybersecurity. Its structured approach aids organizations in defining cybersecurity-related tasks, skills, and competencies required for a successful workforce.

The NICE Framework and the Color Wheel

Just as colors combine to form a harmonious spectrum, the NICE Framework brings together diverse work roles to fortify the digital realm. In this chapter, I explain each of the primary and secondary colors and relate them to four major groups: builders, breakers, defenders, and bakers.

In the following chapters, I embark on a journey to relate NICE Framework work roles to the primary and secondary colors of the color wheel, unveiling a creative perspective on the intricacies of cybersecurity roles and their interconnectedness. I then augment the NICE work roles with sample jobs that exist in the industry but are omitted by the NICE Framework by name (either accidentally or because they are assumed to be subsumed as part of one of the NICE work roles).

April Wright's presentation at the BlackHat USA 2017 conference introduced the concept of the Information Security Color Wheel, a visual framework that helps organizations determine the appropriate levels of security measures based on the sensitivity of their data and systems. The color wheel analogy offers a simplified and effective way to communicate security requirements and priorities to stakeholders within an organization. Louis Cremen, a software developer turned security professional, added to Ms. Wright's color wheel concept by including and blending developers into the infosec circle. The world of information security is dominated by two main groups: red and blue. See Figure 2.1.

The red team is made up of employees or contractors hired to be *breakers*. These ethical hackers work to find security vulnerabilities that a malicious actor could exploit. Their complement, the blue team, are *defenders*. They are responsible for protecting an organization with cybersecurity defenses, such as firewalls and other intrusion prevention systems. As you'll learn later, combining red and blue teams creates a purple team effect, which can exist independently or as part of either a red or blue team, but more on that later.

When Mr. Cremen added the yellow team to the color wheel, he primarily referred to software engineers. Undoubtedly, software engineers are the largest and arguably most influential group in this color slice; however, I prefer to include other types of developers too—for example, IT systems architects, network designers, engineers, and so on. I refer to this group as *builders*. These are people who design and construct software, systems, and integrations that make enterprises more efficient. Their focus is often on implementing requirements (features), and a major pressure point for this group is delivery timelines. With respect to quality, the focus tends to be on functionality, usability, reliability, and performance. Security is a natural add-on to their quality considerations. Further combining red or blue into these yellow teams creates the emerging secondary cyber colors of green and orange. I discuss each of those separately in the coming chapters.

Figure 2.1 Ed Adams cyber color wheel

For all the building, breaking, and defending going on in any given enterprise, there needs to be some form of guiderails. These recipes are provided by a group I refer to as *bakers*. These are the people who collect, collate, and disseminate the security and privacy requirements placed upon the enterprise. These requirements can

The Many Colors of Cybersecurity

be derived from customers, regulators, laws, compliance mandates, and other forms of governance. This is a critically important and often overlooked role for cybersecurity. Job seekers who want to be in cyber but don't want a heavily technical role should look to be a baker. There is a heavy focus on risk assessment, compliance management, and security oversight. Privacy has emerged as a strong force in this group as well, fueled by the omnipresence of laws like the *General Data Protection Regulation* (GDPR) and the *California Consumer Privacy Act* (CCPA). Privacy implications for builders and defenders are highly relevant and far too often ignored or misunderstood. Bakers are associated with the color of a kitchen apron— white. They sit at the center of my color wheel because they touch every other color in some manner.

At the end of 2022, *Cybersecurity Magazine* published an article titled "50 Cybersecurity Titles That Every Job Seeker Should Know About" (see `https://cybersecurityventures.com/50-cyberse curity-titles-that-every-job-seeker-should-know-about`) that does a good job of capturing some of the most frequently used job titles. Here they are in alphabetical order with a terse description of what each does:

- **Application security administrator:** Keeps software/apps safe and secure
- **Artificial intelligence security specialist:** Uses AI to combat cybercrime
- **Automotive security engineer:** Protects cars from cyber intrusions
- **Blockchain developer/engineer:** Codes the future of secure transactions
- **Blue team member:** Designs defensive measures/hardens operating systems

- **Bug bounty hunter:** Freelance hackers who find defects and exploits in code
- **Chief information security officer (CISO):** Head honcho of cybersecurity
- **Chief security officer (CSO):** Heads up all physical/info/cybersecurity
- **Cloud security architect:** Secures the apps and data in the cloud
- **Counterespionage analyst:** Thwarts cyber spies from hostile nation states
- **Cryptanalyst:** Deciphers coded messages without a cryptographic key
- **Cryptographer:** Develops systems to encrypt sensitive information
- **Cyber insurance policy specialist:** Consults on cyber risk and liability protection
- **Cyber intelligence specialist:** Analyzes cyber threats and defends against them
- **Cyber operations specialist:** Conducts offensive cyberspace operations
- **Cybercrime investigator:** Solves crimes conducted in cyberspace
- **Cybersecurity hardware engineer:** Develops security for computer hardware
- **Cybersecurity lawyer:** Attorney focused on info/cybersecurity and cybercrime
- **Cybersecurity scrum master:** Watches over and protects the data

- **Cybersecurity software developer/engineer:** Bakes security into applications

- **Data privacy officer:** Ensures legal compliance related to data protection

- **Data recovery specialist:** Recovers hacked data from digital devices

- **Data security analyst:** Protects information on computers and networks

- **Digital forensics analyst:** Examines data containing evidence of cybercrimes

- **Disaster recovery specialist:** Plans for and responds to data and system catastrophes

- **Ethical/white hat hacker:** Performs lawful security testing and evaluation

- **Governance, compliance, and risk (GRC) manager:** Oversees risk management

- **Incident responder:** First response to cyber intrusions and data breaches

- **Industrial Internet of Things (IIoT) security specialist:** Protects industrial control systems

- **Information assurance analyst:** Identifies risks to information systems

- **Information security analyst:** Plans and carries out infosecurity measures

- **Information security manager/director:** Oversees an IT security team

- **Internet of Things (IoT) security specialist:** Protects network-connected devices

- **Intrusion detection analyst:** Uses security tools to find targeted attacks

- **IT security architect:** Implements network and computer security

- **Malware analyst:** Detects and remediates malicious software

- **Mobile security engineer:** Implements security for mobile phones and devices

- **Network security administrator:** Secures networks from internal and external threats

- **Penetration tester (pentester):** Performs authorized and simulated cyberattacks

- **Public key infrastructure (PKI) analyst:** Manages secure transfer of digital information

- **Red team member:** Participates in real-world cyberattack simulations

- **Security auditor:** Conducts audits on an organization's information systems

- **Security awareness training specialist:** Trains employees on cyber threats

- **Security operations center (SOC) analyst:** Coordinates and reports on cyber incidents

- **Security operations center (SOC) manager:** Oversees all SOC personnel

- **Source code auditor:** Analyzes software code to find bugs, defects, and breaches

- **Supervisory Control and Data Acquisition (SCADA) security analyst:** Secures critical infrastructures

- **Threat hunter:** Searches networks to detect and isolate advanced threats

- **Virus technician:** Detects and remediates computer viruses and malware

- **Vulnerability assessor:** Finds exploits in systems and applications

Every one of these jobs fits into one of the six color slices discussed in this book (and some bleed into more than one). It might be a fun exercise for you to color-code them once you've read the next few chapters. Regardless, this list plus the 50+ work roles in the NICE Framework and the additional titles I provide in the coming chapters, will give you a comprehensive understanding of the myriad of opportunities that abound in cybersecurity.

Cybersecurity Jobs Not on the Color Wheel

I would be remiss if I didn't discuss the cybersecurity job opportunities that exist outside the world of builders, breakers, defenders, and bakers. The cybersecurity industry has witnessed exponential growth in recent years as the digital landscape continues to evolve, with cyber threats becoming more sophisticated and pervasive. As organizations prioritize protecting their digital assets, cybersecurity companies have emerged as vital players in the fight against cybercrime. Beyond the realm of cybersecurity experts and technical professionals, these companies offer a wide range of career opportunities for individuals specializing in sales, marketing, technical support, and customer success. These diverse career paths available for professionals in the cybersecurity industry can be some of the most rewarding. I do not delve into these jobs in detail, like I do for those on the color wheel; therefore, I want to give them an appropriate amount of attention in this preambulatory chapter.

Cybersecurity encompasses strategies, technologies, and practices designed to protect digital systems, networks, and data from theft, damage, and unauthorized access. With the growing volume and complexity of cyber threats, businesses, government agencies, and individuals require robust cybersecurity solutions to safeguard their digital assets. Relevant to note is that just as often, those chartered with protecting the enterprise are not highly technical. They are often business-oriented managers and leaders in need of solutions that are easy to understand, implement, and operate for their teams. Cybersecurity companies play a critical role in helping organizations stay ahead of evolving threats, and like most companies, there are jobs in customer-facing roles that are paramount to the success of the cybersecurity provider and its customers.

Sales

Consider these jobs that fall within the sales realm but that have aspects of cybersecurity built into them. These work roles typically promote and advocate for the products and services offered by a cybersecurity company:

- **Sales representative/sales account executive:** Sales professionals in cybersecurity companies are responsible for identifying potential clients, understanding their security needs, and promoting relevant products or services. They build relationships, negotiate contracts, and work closely with technical teams to provide tailored solutions. Given the complexity of cybersecurity, sales representatives often require a strong understanding of the industry's terminology and trends.

- **Sales engineer/solutions engineer:** Sales engineers bridge the gap between technical expertise and sales efforts. They assist sales teams by demonstrating how cybersecurity solutions work and how they can address specific client challenges. Sales engineers need a deep understanding of the company's product portfolio and the technical acumen to communicate complex concepts effectively.

- **Sales manager/director:** Sales managers and directors oversee sales teams, set sales targets, and develop strategies to achieve revenue goals. They collaborate with other departments, such as marketing and product development, to align sales efforts with the company's objectives. In the cybersecurity sector, they also play a crucial role in staying updated on industry trends and competitor offerings.

Marketing

Consider these jobs that typically fall within the marketing realm but that have aspects of cybersecurity built into them. These work roles often are jobs for cybersecurity companies; however, there are also plenty of cyber-focused marketing roles for larger companies that could be related to an "office of product security" or marketing products that have security features as differentiators. For example, a company like Honeywell Connected Enterprise has the following:

- **Product marketing manager:** Product marketing managers in cybersecurity companies are responsible for crafting messaging and positioning for security products or services. They conduct market research, analyze competitors, and develop marketing strategies that resonate with target audiences. A deep understanding of the cybersecurity landscape is essential to effectively communicate the value of security solutions.

- **Content marketing specialist:** Content marketing specialists create valuable content, such as blog posts, whitepapers, videos, and webinars, to educate and engage potential customers. They must have a solid grasp of cybersecurity concepts and trends to produce relevant and informative content that establishes the company as a trusted authority in the field.

- **Digital marketing manager:** Digital marketing managers leverage various online channels, including social media, email marketing, search engine optimization (SEO), and paid advertising, to promote cybersecurity products and services. They analyze data and metrics to optimize campaigns and generate leads.

Technical Support

Consider these jobs that typically fall within technical support but that have aspects of cybersecurity. There are two distinct types of jobs I mention here—work roles that provide technical support for a cybersecurity product where knowledge of cyber is useful and perhaps necessary, and work roles that incorporate cybersecurity considerations as a value-added skill. The latter would be mindful of exposing sensitive customer data and would question the systems used for managing and sharing that information if they were cyber-informed. Here are a couple of sample titles:

- **Technical support specialist/engineer:** Technical support specialists or engineers assist customers and end users in implementing, troubleshooting, and maintaining cybersecurity solutions. They diagnose technical issues, provide solutions, and ensure a positive customer experience. Technical support professionals need a strong technical background and a deep understanding of the company's products.

- **Security analyst (customer-facing):** Some cybersecurity companies employ security analysts who work directly with customers to interpret security alerts, investigate incidents, and provide recommendations for improving security postures. They play a crucial role in helping clients understand and respond to potential threats.

Customer Success

Consider these jobs that typically fall within the customer success realm but that have aspects of cybersecurity. Similar to technical support, these roles could relate to a cybersecurity product, or they could incorporate cyber-awareness as a means to make the employee more valuable and enhance the employer's overall cybersecurity hygiene in the process:

- **Customer success manager:** Customer success managers build and maintain strong relationships with clients, ensuring their ongoing satisfaction and success with the company's products or services. They work closely with customers to understand their goals, address challenges, and maximize the value they receive. In the cybersecurity industry, customer success managers may also assist in creating security strategies and best practices.

- **Onboarding specialist:** Onboarding specialists are responsible for guiding new customers through the process of implementing cybersecurity solutions. They ensure that clients have a seamless and positive experience during the initial setup and configuration phase.

- **Renewals specialist:** Renewals specialists focus on retaining existing customers by managing contract renewals and ensuring that clients continue to receive value from their cybersecurity investments. They may also identify opportunities for upselling or cross-selling additional products or services.

Skills Needed for Jobs Not on the Color Wheel

Jobs in sales, marketing, support, and customer success require certain highly valuable skills and qualifications. I list them here in order of importance based on my personal experience and that I gleaned from the many interviews I conducted during the research phase for this book:

- **Communication skills:** Effective communication is crucial, whether it's conveying technical information to nontechnical clients, collaborating with cross-functional teams, or creating compelling marketing content.

- **Problem-solving abilities:** Cybersecurity professionals often encounter challenging and evolving threats. The ability to analyze problems, develop solutions, and adapt to new circumstances is essential.

- **Willingness to learn:** The cybersecurity landscape is constantly changing, with new threats and technology stacks to deal with. That alone requires an open mind to learn; but there are also customer-specific problems that don't necessarily relate to a cyber threat or solution. Empathy with the desire to understand and resolve these problems will take you very far in your cyber career.

- **Customer-centric mindset:** Those in customer-facing roles, such as sales, technical support, and customer success, should prioritize customer satisfaction and success. Building and maintaining strong customer relationships is key.

- **Technical aptitude:** Some roles, especially in technical support and sales engineering, require a strong technical background to assist customers with complex security solutions.

- **Cybersecurity knowledge:** Professionals in these roles benefit from a foundational understanding of cybersecurity principles, threats, and best practices. This knowledge helps them communicate effectively with clients and colleagues and make informed decisions.

Challenges for All Jobs

Working in the cybersecurity industry offers exciting opportunities, but it also comes with unique challenges.

- **Rapid technological advancements:** The cybersecurity landscape evolves rapidly, with new threats and technologies emerging regularly. Professionals must stay up-to-date with industry trends and adapt to new challenges.

- **Cyber skills gap:** There is a shortage of cybersecurity professionals globally. This presents both an opportunity for job seekers and a challenge for organizations struggling to fill cybersecurity roles. You may be asked to stretch yourself into an uncomfortable/unfamiliar role. This can also present good career opportunities for rapid advancement if you are properly motivated and proven to be successful.

- **Diverse career paths:** The cybersecurity field offers a wide range of career paths, allowing professionals to specialize in areas that align with their interests and skills.

- **Ethical considerations:** Professionals working in cybersecurity must navigate ethical dilemmas, especially when addressing privacy concerns and data protection.

- **Diversity and inclusion:** The cybersecurity industry is not a particularly diverse one in terms of race, gender, sexual identity, religion, and other demographics. It is improving, but you need to be mindful of these facts as you enter or transition into the field.

The cybersecurity industry is a dynamic and vital sector, and it offers a plethora of career opportunities for individuals with diverse skills and backgrounds. Whether you're passionate about sales, marketing, technical support, customer success, or other business profession, you can find a fulfilling career at a cybersecurity company. As cyber threats continue to evolve, the demand for skilled professionals in these roles is expected to remain strong, making the industry an attractive destination for those seeking meaningful and impactful careers.

Summary

In the tapestry of cybersecurity, a spectrum of roles and responsibilities merge to create a cohesive and secure digital world. By drawing parallels between the NICE Framework work roles and the primary and secondary colors of the color wheel, we uncover a vivid and interconnected landscape. Primary colors mirror foundational roles such as Analyze, Secure, Operate, and Maintain, which form the bedrock of cybersecurity operations. Secondary colors highlight interdisciplinary roles such as Oversee and Govern, Support and Operations, and Innovate, emphasizing collaboration, harmony, guidance, and innovation.

Just as the colors on the wheel blend seamlessly, work roles need to complement and support each other to create a holistic approach to cybersecurity. The analogy between colors and roles serves as a reminder that cybersecurity is not a solitary endeavor; rather, it is a collective effort that requires the expertise and cooperation of various professionals. As the digital landscape continues to evolve, this unique perspective underscores the intricate dance of colors and roles that shape the ever-changing cybersecurity world.

To continue the analogy, if the colors represent cybersecurity functions in various jobs, then the jobs that sustain and enable those functions make up the canvas itself. Often unnoticed, these are the roles in sales, marketing, and support that bring cybersecurity solutions to market, equip consumers with the tools and processes needed to implement cyber solutions, and ensure the proper deployment and use of those products and services. They, too, represent good career opportunities that can be explored.

By juxtaposing the NICE Framework's cybersecurity work roles with the primary and secondary colors of the color wheel, you gain a unique perspective on the diverse roles that collectively shape the cybersecurity landscape. Overlaid with references to job functions that exist in many businesses and organizations, this perspective should provide a clear vision for both job seekers and hirers. I hope this analogy not only simplifies the complex world of cybersecurity but also underscores the importance of clarity in job descriptions, teamwork, and strategic planning for the safety of our digital assets.

Chapter 3

Primary Colors: Foundational Cybersecurity Work Roles

This chapter looks at three of the four major groups in the world of cybersecurity as described in the preceding chapter. I discuss the builders, breakers, and defenders. The fourth group, the bakers, has its own chapter following the discussion of the primary and secondary color groups.

Red: Analyze and Attack

At the heart of cybersecurity lies the ability to dissect, understand, and respond to threats. Analogous to the color red, which symbolizes attention and alertness, the Analyze work roles in the NICE Framework focus on identifying vulnerabilities, analyzing attack vectors, and deciphering complex data. Security analysts and incident responders exemplify the vigilant nature of red by scrutinizing security incidents and rapidly responding to mitigate threats. Just as the color red captures immediate attention, Analyze roles highlight the critical importance of identifying and addressing vulnerabilities in real time.

Red work roles are at the core of cybersecurity operations. Individuals in these roles are fundamentally attackers, which is why I use the term *breakers*. They identify vulnerabilities by conducting attacks on the IT systems and applications that run their organization. Many consider them ethical hackers. They embody the approach of offensive security needed to dissect complex cyber threats by simulating those threats in safe environments. Red teamers demonstrate their role in understanding potential security breaches by finding flaws that were missed during the build phase.

The most common job in this color slice is the penetration tester (aka pentester). You won't find this job listed in the NICE Framework, much to my chagrin, but it is a popular one in the industry. There are many variants of pentester job titles in practice. Some include the word *engineer* in the title, and others specify the platform or technology specialization required, for example, application security engineer, mobile app penetration tester, and network penetration tester. Other job titles use qualifiers to denote seniority and specify only the type of work, for example, principal consultant offensive security and associate offensive security engineer. In general, if the job title is only penetration tester, it can be assumed to mean network-level testing and not specific to the application layer, such as web, mobile, or cloud applications. You may also find the job titles ethical hacker and, increasingly, red team member. Closely related to these (and sometimes performing nearly the same tasks) are vulnerability assessment jobs. You often find the term *vulnerability assessment* in job titles used in the U.S. government and banking industries more so than others.

The Strategic Art of Red Teaming: Fortifying Cyber Defense Through Simulation

The field of cybersecurity is a constant battleground, where organizations must anticipate and counteract a wide array of threats to safeguard their digital assets. In this dynamic environment, traditional defensive measures alone might not suffice. Enter red teaming, a powerful approach that enables organizations to adopt the perspective attacks of adversaries and simulate real-world attacks. These attacks are well documented in the MITRE ATT&CK Framework (see `https://attack.mitre.org`). I strongly recommend reading and practicing the attacks listed therein to anyone interested in being a red team member of a cybersecurity organization.

Red teaming is not just a security exercise; it's a strategic mindset that challenges the status quo. It involves forming a dedicated team, often referred to as the *red team*, to simulate the actions, tactics, and techniques of potential adversaries. The objective is to identify vulnerabilities, weaknesses, and gaps in an organization's defenses by replicating real-world attack scenarios. Unlike traditional penetration testing, where specific vulnerabilities are targeted, red teaming encompasses a holistic approach that mimics the broader actions of cyber attackers.

The red team conducts thorough reconnaissance, devises attack strategies, and executes attacks against the organization's infrastructure, applications, and personnel. The ultimate goal is to emulate the perspective of a malicious actor, thereby providing organizations with insights into their own security posture and vulnerabilities. Red teaming helps organizations identify potential blind spots, evaluate their security measures, and ultimately strengthen their cyber defense strategies.

Red teaming is an important element of cyber defense. Traditional security assessments might overlook certain vulnerabilities due to the limited scope of testing. Red teaming takes a comprehensive approach, probing various attack vectors and potential weak points that might otherwise go unnoticed. By identifying hidden vulnerabilities, organizations can proactively address potential entry points for cyber threats.

Benefits of Red Teaming

The realistic attack simulation that red teams mimic are scenarios the organization are likely to face, providing a realistic understanding of how adversaries operate. This approach helps the enterprise anticipate potential attack vectors, techniques, and procedures, enabling them to fine-tune their defenses and response strategies accordingly. A beneficial side effect is the cultivation of a proactive security mindset. Rather than waiting for attackers to exploit vulnerabilities, red teaming empowers organizations to take a proactive stance. By simulating attacks before they occur, organizations can identify weaknesses in advance and implement measures to mitigate potential risks.

This also enhances their incident response capabilities and speed. Through red teaming exercises, organizations develop a deeper understanding of how attackers infiltrate their systems and networks. This knowledge is invaluable when it comes to incident response. Organizations can refine their incident response plans, develop effective mitigation strategies, and reduce the time it takes to detect and neutralize threats. This is the first step toward continuous improvement. Red teaming isn't a one-time exercise; it's an ongoing process that aligns with the dynamic nature of cybersecurity. Regular red teaming assessments enable organizations to continuously evolve their defenses, adapting to emerging threats and staying ahead of attackers.

My final comment on the benefits of red teaming revolves around risk management and resource allocation. Red teaming helps organizations make more informed decisions about their limited resources of time, money, and people. More effective identification of critical vulnerabilities that require immediate attention ensures that investments are targeted toward addressing the most pressing security concerns. This plays directly into strengthening the security culture of the organization as it fosters security awareness across multiple teams. Employees become more vigilant about potential threats and learn to recognize unusual activities that might indicate an attack. This heightened awareness contributes to a collective effort to maintain cyber hygiene.

Red Team Work Roles That Align with NICE

The work roles from the NICE Framework that most closely align with the concept of red teaming are those that involve offensive security strategies, vulnerability assessment, and analyzing IT systems. Their titles are misaligned with the commonly used ones in industry, listed previously, but they are useful for comparative purposes. The job summaries in the following sections, and particularly the skills and tasks listed for each, make for a more complete and accurate understanding. Note the specialty area abbreviation for each work role—SP = Securely Provision, AN = Analyze, CO = Collect and Operate, and so forth.

Secure Software Assessor (SP)

Secure software assessors conceptualize, design, procure, and/or build secure IT systems, with responsibility for aspects of system and/or network development. They develop and write/code new (or modify existing) computer applications, software, or specialized utility programs following software assurance best practices. They analyze the security of new or existing computer applications, software, or specialized utility programs and provide actionable results.

Security Control Assessor (SP)

Security control assessors oversee, evaluate, and support the documentation, validation, assessment, and authorization processes necessary to ensure that existing and new IT systems meet the organization's cybersecurity and risk requirements. They ensure appropriate treatment of risk, compliance, and assurance from internal and external perspectives.

They conduct independent comprehensive assessments of the management, operational, and technical security controls and control enhancements employed within or inherited by an IT system to determine the overall effectiveness of the controls.

Exploitation Analyst (AN)

Exploitation analysts examine vulnerabilities in software, systems, and networks to determine their potential for exploitation by malicious actors. They assess the impact and risk associated with vulnerabilities and provide recommendations for mitigation.

Vulnerability Assessment Analyst (VA)

Vulnerability analysts analyze system vulnerabilities, assess their potential impact, and provide recommendations for mitigation. They work to ensure that systems are patched and updated to protect against known vulnerabilities. They analyze collected information to identify vulnerabilities and potential for exploitation.

Cyber Operator (CO)

Cyber operators, or as they are more commonly known in the industry, cyber operations engineers, design and implement offensive security strategies, including red teaming exercises. They use their expertise to develop simulated attacks that mimic real-world threats, helping organizations identify weaknesses and enhance their defense strategies. They provide specialized denial and deception operations and collection of cybersecurity information that may be used to develop intelligence. They perform activities to gather evidence on criminal or foreign intelligence entities to mitigate possible or real-time threats, protect against espionage or insider threats, foreign sabotage, international terrorist activities, or support other intelligence activities. They conduct collection, processing, and/or geolocation of systems to exploit, locate, and/or track targets of interest. They perform network navigation, tactical forensic analysis, and, when directed, execute on-net operations.

Cyber Operations Planner (CO)

Cyber operations planners develop strategies for conducting red team exercises and other offensive security operations. They collaborate with various teams to design simulations that challenge an organization's security posture. They also develop detailed plans for the conduct or support of the applicable range of cyber operations through collaboration with other planners, operators, and/or analysts.

Other Red Team Roles

Other offensive security work roles I have seen, particularly in government settings, include the ones that follow.

Cyber Operations Analyst

Cyber operations analysts participate in red teaming exercises by executing simulated attacks and analyzing the effectiveness of an organization's defense mechanisms. They identify vulnerabilities and provide insights for improving cybersecurity practices.

Cyber Operations Incident Responder

Cyber operations incident responders investigate and respond to security incidents, including those identified during red teaming exercises. They analyze attack techniques and tactics to develop effective response strategies.

Cyber Threat Emulation Analyst

Cyber threat analysts emulate cyber threats and attack scenarios to assess an organization's readiness and response capabilities. They simulate realistic attacks and evaluate the effectiveness of security controls and incident response procedures.

Red Team Operator

Red team operators execute red teaming exercises, simulating attacks to identify vulnerabilities and weaknesses in an organization's defenses. They use advanced techniques and tactics to emulate the behaviors of real attackers.

One of the nonprofits in cybersecurity, CSNP (`www.csnp.org`) published a useful (and short) guide on preparing oneself for a career in offensive security/penetration testing/red teaming. It covers the basics but also discusses specific tools and industry certifications to pursue. You can find it here: `www.csnp.org/post/a-career-in-offensive-security-penetration-testing-red-teaming`.

These work roles from the NICE Framework reflect the offensive and adversarial nature of red teaming in cybersecurity. Professionals in these roles focus on identifying vulnerabilities, emulating attack scenarios, and helping organizations improve their cybersecurity posture through proactive assessments and simulations.

A Red Wrap-Up

In a digital landscape characterized by rapidly evolving cyber threats, the strategic approach of red teaming stands as a cornerstone of resilient cyber defense. By adopting the perspective of adversaries, organizations gain a realistic view of their vulnerabilities, anticipate potential threats, and proactively strengthen their security measures.

The insights obtained from red teaming exercises enable organizations to identify hidden weaknesses, enhance incident response capabilities, and foster a culture of security awareness. In the quest for a robust cyber defense strategy, red teaming empowers organizations to challenge assumptions, assess their security posture comprehensively, and remain vigilant against the evolving threat landscape.

Blue: Secure and Defend

Blue signifies stability and trust, characteristics that resonate strongly with the Protect and Defend work roles in the NICE Framework. Cybersecurity professionals in these roles safeguard systems, networks, and data by implementing protective measures such as encryption, access controls, and firewalls. Network security engineers and system administrators, for instance, embody the essence of blue by ensuring the steadfast security of digital assets. Just as the color blue instills a sense of calmness, the Protect and Defend roles instill confidence in users, ensuring them that their information is well-protected.

These roles focus on fortifying systems, networks, and data from external threats. Cybersecurity professionals in this category safeguard digital assets, applying encryption, access controls, and firewalls to shield against unauthorized access. Just as blue symbolizes tranquility, the Secure work roles create a sense of calmness amid the chaotic cyber landscape. Examples of such roles include network security engineers and system administrators.

These are the *defenders* of the enterprise. They construct and maintain resilient defenses around the applications and systems that run the organization. In the digital age, where cyber threats are relentless and increasingly sophisticated, the role of defenders is arguably the most critical in safeguarding digital assets and information. While offensive strategies like red teaming are important, defenders must stand strong to protect against evolving threats. Enter blue teaming, a proactive approach that focuses on enhancing cyber defense strategies and strengthening an organization's ability to detect, respond to, and recover from cyberattacks. The blue team's significance is its cyber defense posture and how it contributes to a more secure digital landscape.

Blue Teaming: Preventing and Responding to Attacks

Blue teaming is the defensive counterpart to red teaming. While red teams simulate adversarial attacks to identify vulnerabilities and weaknesses, blue teams work to develop and implement strategies that prevent, detect, and respond to such attacks. Blue teaming is not just about technology; it encompasses people, processes, and technologies that collectively form a robust defense against cyber threats.

Blue teams focus on proactive threat hunting, continuous monitoring, and incident response planning. They employ tools, technologies, and methodologies to identify and mitigate risks, ensuring that security measures are effective and efficient. Blue teaming is an integral part of building a resilient cyber defense posture by enabling organizations to detect threats early, respond promptly, and minimize the potential impact of cyber incidents.

Common job titles for blue team cybersecurity professionals include information security analyst/officer/manager/administrator, cybersecurity engineer, soc analyst, cyber analyst, security analyst, system security specialist, and cybersecurity monitoring engineer. These are, by far, the most common titles used to describe the people who are responsible for managing an information security program. I refer to them collectively as *infosec professionals*.

Take care to thoroughly review the job description, responsibilities, and expectations to ensure they match precisely with what you desire from that particular job. As hiring managers, multi-use titles are helpful to attract many applicants; however, all too often the responsibilities listed vary wildly for the exact same job title. This is where the knowledge, skills, abilities, and tasks from the NICE Framework can provide utility.

Before I discuss some of the NICE Framework roles for the blue color slice, let me explain some of the benefits blue teams and infosec professionals provide to organizations.

Benefits of Blue Teaming

Proactive threat detection is the epitome of a blue team. It emphasizes proactive threat detection through continuous monitoring of networks, systems, and applications. By monitoring for unusual activities and identifying potential indicators of compromise, blue teams can detect threats before they escalate into full-blown attacks. This leads directly into early incident response. Rapid response to breaches is crucial in minimizing the impact of cyber events. Blue teaming ensures that organizations have well-defined incident response plans in place, allowing them to respond swiftly to threats, contain the damage, and recover data effectively. These plans are routinely tested via simulations, often in partnership with the red team.

One of the long standing tenants of cybersecurity is something known as *defense in depth*, layering defenses atop one another so that if one is breached there is another safety net below it, so to speak. Blue teaming adopts a defense-in-depth approach, where multiple security measures are deployed to protect against a wide range of attack vectors. This approach ensures that if one layer is compromised, other layers provide additional protection, making it harder for attackers to infiltrate. For example, breaching a firewall might allow an attacker to get access to a corporate network; however, once on the network, their actions to scan for targets might

39

trip an intrusion detection system or provoke a credential challenge for authentication. These measures help deter even persistent threat actors.

Blue teams also help optimize security measures. By conducting regular security assessments, vulnerability assessments, and reviewing penetration test reports, blue teams can identify areas where security measures can be improved. This includes patching vulnerabilities, configuring security controls, and fine-tuning access controls. The more automated this process, the more real-time threat intelligence can be gleaned. Blue teaming leverages threat intelligence to stay informed about emerging threats, attack trends, and new attack techniques. This information helps organizations stay ahead of attackers by adapting their defense strategies to counter the latest threats.

Just like their red counterparts, blue teamers build a resilient culture of security for the organization. Blue teaming extends beyond technology to include training, awareness, and education. It stokes this culture of security among employees, making them the first line of defense against social engineering attacks and other cyber threats. This further assists with incident analysis and proactive event learning as the team analyzes past incidents to understand attack patterns, tactics, and techniques. This analysis helps organizations fine-tune their defense strategies and adapt to evolving threat landscapes by preparing their staff accordingly.

Blue teams are also responsible for helping the organization be in compliance. I talk more about governance, risk, and compliance (GRC) jobs later, but those roles depend on the blue team for the data they need to make those informed decisions that guide the organization's data privacy and protection strategies. Many industries are subject to regulatory requirements that mandate robust cybersecurity measures. Blue teaming assists organizations in meeting these compliance requirements by demonstrating effective security practices and incident response capabilities.

Blue Team Work Roles That Align with NICE

By my account, nearly 50 percent of the NICE work roles align to blue. The work roles from the NICE Framework that most closely align with the concept of blue teaming are those related to cybersecurity defense, incident response, and proactive monitoring. Here are the top 10 work roles that align with blue teaming:

- **Executive cyber leadership (OG):** Supervise, manage, and/ or lead work and workers performing cyber and cyber-related and/or cyber operations work. For many organizations, this is the chief information security officer (CISO). Depending on the type of organization, you may also see chief product security officer (CPSO), chief data security officer (CDSO), and similar C-level security officer titles.

- **Privacy officers (OG):** Develop and oversee the privacy compliance program and privacy program staff, supporting privacy compliance, governance/policy, and incident response needs of privacy and security executives and their teams. This is also commonly referred to as a data privacy officer/executive/ director/manager.

- **Cyber instructor/curriculum developers (OG):** Develop and conduct training or education of personnel within the cyber domain. Also develop, plan, coordinate, and evaluate cyber training/education courses, methods, and techniques based on instructional needs. This is commonly referred to as security awareness manager/lead in most organizations. Increasingly, I also see references to titles akin to security culture officer.

- **Cyber workforce managers (OG):** Develop policies and plans to advocate for changes that support organizational cyberspace initiatives with required changes or enhancements to staff skills. Develop cyberspace workforce plans, strategies, and guidance to support cyberspace workforce hours, personnel, training, and education requirements and to address changes to cyberspace policy, doctrine, materiel, force structure, and education and training requirements.

- **Cybercrime investigators (IN):** Investigate cybersecurity events or crimes related to information technology systems, networks, and digital evidence. Apply tactics, techniques, and procedures for a full range of investigative tools and processes that include, but are not limited to, interview and interrogation techniques, surveillance, counter surveillance, and surveillance detection. They also appropriately balance the benefits of prosecution versus intelligence gathering. Identify, collect, examine, and preserve evidence using controlled and documented analytical and investigative techniques.

- **Cyber defense incident responders (PD):** Responsible for identifying, mitigating, and responding to cybersecurity incidents. They analyze security alerts, investigate breaches, and work to minimize the impact of security breaches. This rapid-response job reacts to crises or urgent situations to mitigate immediate and potential threats. They use mitigation, preparedness, and recovery approaches to maximize survival of life, preservation of property, and information security.

- **Cyber defense analysts (PD):** They analyze network traffic, help to investigate security incidents, and develop strategies to protect against cyber threats. They also identify vulnerabilities and recommend remediation measures. They do this by using data collected from a variety of cyber defense tools—including IDS alerts, firewalls, and network traffic logs—to analyze events that occur in their environments for the purposes of mitigating threats.

- **Cyber defense infrastructure support specialists (PD):** CDISS professionals provide technical support for cybersecurity tools and infrastructure. They ensure that security systems are properly configured and operational to defend against threats. This means monitoring networks for unauthorized activities as well as testing, maintaining, and administering the infrastructure hardware and software that collects cyber intelligence.

- **Target/language/all-source analysts (AN):** These roles (there are several combined here) analyze data from one or multiple sources to prepare a target environment, respond to requests for information, and submit intelligence in support of planning and operations. They also perform highly specialized review and evaluation of incoming cybersecurity information to determine its usefulness for intelligence, and, where appropriate, apply spoken language, cultural, and other expertise needed to interpret the intel.

- **Information systems security manager (OG):** ISSMs oversee the security of an organization's information systems, ensuring compliance with security policies, managing security incidents, and implementing defensive strategies. They may oversee a cybersecurity program that could span strategic, personnel management, policy enforcement, emergency planning, and security awareness.

Other Blue Team Work Roles

There are other common titles NICE does not include specifically that are worth knowing.

- **Security operations center (SOC) analysts:** They monitor network traffic, detect security incidents, and respond to threats in real time. They play a critical role in maintaining the security of an organization's systems and networks. This is a very popular role in cybersecurity and offers entry-level opportunities to learn and grow one's career. SOC analysts need to be ethical, curious, and detail oriented, because they are responsible for monitoring many systems simultaneously and raising appropriate alerts, even for perceived insider threats.

- **Security engineers:** They design, implement, and manage security solutions to protect systems and networks. They work to prevent unauthorized access, monitor for anomalies, and respond to security incidents. This is a more generic job title that can encompass many different tasks and areas of responsibility. Job hirers use this title with caution, and, if possible, cross-reference NICE knowledge, skills, and abilities (KSAs) with the responsibilities and experience you require for the job in question. Otherwise, you are likely to get mismatched applicants for your job opening. *Security engineer* is an overloaded term in the industry; therefore, more precision when describing roles and responsibilities is highly recommended.

- **Security control assessor/validators:** They assess the effectiveness of security controls and measures to ensure they align with organizational policies and industry standards. This is intended to be an independent, comprehensive assessment of the management, operational, and technical security controls that are employed within an IT system to determine the overall effectiveness of said controls. It is often as defined in a standard such as PCI-DSS or NIST SP 800-37.

- **Information security:** Also known as infosec, this catchall phrase mostly refers to blue teams, but because it is used in many different work environments, take the extra time to learn what is meant by infosec in the particular organization you're considering. Network defenders are the most commonly thought of job in infosec teams; they focus on safeguarding networks from cyber threats by monitoring network traffic, detecting unauthorized access, and implementing security measures.

These work roles from the NICE Framework and the others I mention reflect the defensive and protective nature of blue teaming/ infosec professional in cybersecurity. Practitioners in these roles do the important work of maintaining the security and integrity of systems, networks, applications, and data, while also responding effectively to cyber incidents and ensuring compliance with security standards.

Blue Skies Ahead

As the digital landscape continues to evolve, the role of blue teams in cyber defense becomes increasingly critical. Blue teaming represents the vigilant defenders who work tirelessly to protect digital assets and sensitive information from cyber threats. By emphasizing proactive threat detection, early incident response, defense-in-depth strategies, and a resilient security culture, blue teaming ensures that organizations are well-prepared to face and mitigate cyber risks.

In a world where cyberattacks are not a matter of "if" but "when," blue teaming stands as a beacon of resilience, enabling organizations to detect, respond to, and recover from cyber incidents effectively. By adopting a proactive and collaborative approach to cyber defense, this blue color slice contributes to a more secure digital landscape, safeguarding the integrity, confidentiality, and availability of data and resources.

Yellow: Build and Maintain

The color yellow is akin to the Securely Provision (SP) work roles in the NICE Framework. The Securely Provision category in the NICE

Primary Colors: Foundational Cybersecurity Work Roles

Framework focuses on ensuring that cybersecurity is an integral part of an organization's information systems, infrastructure, and processes as they are being defined, designed, built, tested, and deployed. This category encompasses activities related to the procurement, design, development, and implementation of secure systems and applications. It is fundamental in building a strong foundation for cybersecurity by addressing potential vulnerabilities early in the development life cycle.

Roles within the Securely Provision category typically involve creating and maintaining secure environments, ensuring that security is embedded into all aspects of an organization's operations, and complying with relevant cybersecurity policies and regulations.

It is important to note that, unlike red teams and blue teams, all the other color slices do *not* have security as their primary job function. The "breakers" in red and "defenders" in blue work diligently to secure and protect the IT systems and applications constructed by the "builders" in yellow teams.

Introducing Yellow Teams

I like to use the analogy of building a house when discussing yellow teams. These builders are responsible for five key phases of development:

- Definition
- Design
- Construction
- Testing
- Deployment and maintenance

Consider the house analogy. First, you must define what will be built, for example, a four-bedroom Colonial with 2.5 baths and 2,000 square feet of living space, as a rudimentary example. Next, an architect will create a blueprint (perhaps several different options that meet the defined requirements), and you choose which to use. Then, a team assembles the house from the ground up. This team will have different roles: framers if it's a wood-framed house, plumbers, electricians, masons, excavation specialists, roofers, and so forth. They implement the design using their particular special skills. Next, the house must be tested for proper functionality and safety before it can be occupied, so you bring in inspectors...building inspectors, plumbing inspectors, electric inspectors, and so forth. Once the house is deemed fit for human living, an occupancy permit/certification is obtained, and people move in. But that's not the end of the process. Things break, so they need to be fixed. Certain things need to be maintained to ensure they don't cause problems. The lawn may need to be mowed, the house repainted, roofing shingles repaired. This is exactly what happens with IT systems and software applications. And each phase has specific job functions, titles, and responsibilities associated with it.

The Yellow Team Paradox

The vast majority of work roles and responsibilities in the yellow slice do *not* have security incorporated into the title, skills, or tasks. I believe security is a fundamental aspect of IT system quality, similar to functionality, performance, reliability, and so on, but it isn't taught that way in universities, nor is it generally expected from builders. Consider Figure 3.1. I created this more than 15 years ago to illustrate how security is just another aspect of IT/software quality. It is still perfectly relevant today.

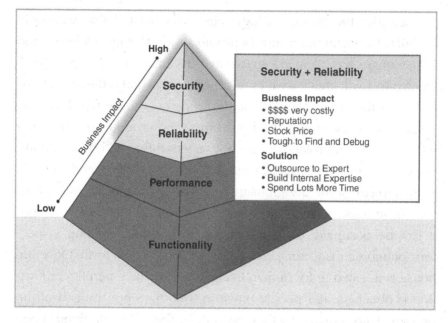

Figure 3.1 Security as an aspect of quality

The most common scenario—both today and when I entered the cybersecurity world 20 years ago—is that the builders build and expect the defenders to secure and protect. This has caused massive problems in both culture and technical inability to properly defend, especially when it comes to software systems. Most defenders (the blue team) come from a world of IT, networks, access controls, and policies that define the dos and don'ts of security. However, the way software applications are made, the focus is mainly on features and time to release. This can often be in direct opposition to controls intended to secure, albeit not intentionally. Security is often seen as an extra (and sometimes unnecessary) step in the software and IT system development world. This is an onerous burden or tax placed upon the builders. In fact, it should be quite the opposite; a security focus while building can and should enable faster release cycles and higher overall quality.

Once development teams consider security vulnerabilities to be the same as they do other "bugs" or defects found in their code and applications, they inherently understand that eradicating them earlier means less time fixing problems and more time building features (their ultimate goal). A development team would never accept an e-commerce application they built if it took four minutes to process a credit card transaction. They'd view this as failure of a core requirement and log it as a performance bug. In his book titled *How to Break Software Security*, Dr. James A. Whittaker drew a simple yet very illustrative diagram that shows how security bugs differ from other types of bugs. I offer a facsimile of that original diagram in Figure 3.2, as it is still as relevant today as when he created it 20+ years ago.

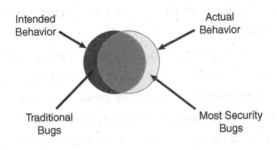

Figure 3.2 How security bugs differ from other types of bugs

Consider the dark blue circle in Figure 3.2 (the intended behavior) the system specification. In the house analogy, this is the set of requirements (4-bedroom, 2.5-bathroom Colonial, with 2000 square feet of living space). IT systems and applications also have specs—architects and developers design and build according to those specs. However, humans aren't perfect, so the actual house comes out a little bit different, just like software applications might turn out differently than the spec intended (actual behavior in Figure 3.2). Traditional bugs like functionality or performance—for example, that

Primary Colors: Foundational Cybersecurity Work Roles

e-commerce site taking four minutes to process a transaction—are shown in the crescent shape on the left. These are things the application is supposed to do but doesn't. A tester would check the entire set of requirements, and if something doesn't meet a particular specification, they would log a bug (a defect). The white crescent shape on the right represents things the application does but is not supposed to. For example, it might not encrypt the credit card data for that e-commerce transaction, or it might display information provided by the user on a confirmation page without sanitizing that input. These are security bugs. But, most testers miss these bugs (especially during the building phase) for the simple reason that they don't look for them. Testing is often driven by the spec; if the spec includes security requirements, they can be validated. But if there are no security requirements, chances are there won't be security elements in the design, nor during construction.

Builders are our yellow team, and the biggest group inside the build team are developers with titles like software engineer, system developer, programmer, and very commonly just developer. We established that a developer's focus is on functionality and delivering that functionality as quickly as possible. Developers typically don't think about whether they've done something securely unless it's defined as part of the requirements and/or design. Most commonly, a developer becomes aware of a security flaw when they receive a bug report from a red team exercise, usually referred to as a *penetration test*. Even more dire is the situation where a security flaw is reported as part of a breach discovered by the blue team.

Now consider the fact that most organizations are adopting and building software and other technology (think blockchain, cloud, and IoT) faster than they learn how to secure it (or even security test or defend it). Presently there are as many cloud misconfiguration security flaws found as there are security holes in the system itself that's deployed to the cloud. At the core of both of these issues are the people or group who build and then operate that system.

The bottom line: This group needs upskilling with respect to security. If you're already part of a development/build team, adding security skills to your repertoire makes you much more valuable. It will enhance your position at your present employer and make you more attractive for promotion or career opportunities elsewhere. If you're an executive, hiring manager, HR leader, or head of some engineering/product group, add security elements to your job descriptions and desired skills.

Yellow Team Work Roles

This section examines some of the titles on the yellow team, using those same five steps previously referenced:

- **Definition:** Here you'll find product manager, program manager, business analyst, product owner, requirements manager.

- **Design:** This is the world of architects. Software, cloud, system, IT, and other architects operate as designers or design engineers and may focus on user interface (UI), user experience (UX), or the components of a system (blueprint) that take the requirements and create the intended effect. This design is then handed to the developers for implementation.

- **Construction:** As mentioned, this includes software engineer, system developer, programmer, and commonly just developer.

- **Testing:** This is the realm of quality assurance (QA), quality engineering (QE), test engineer, developer in test, and verification and validation (V&V). Also, software assurance is often seen in government segments.

- **Deployment and maintenance:** This is the broadest group in terms of titles. Everything from build/release engineer to IT engineer, DevOps engineer, site reliability engineer, and system administrators can be found in this phase.

In the more modern world of DevOps, developers are spinning up servers and IT is managing infrastructure as code. With these new responsibilities come new security skill requirements. Leaders need to lay out a detailed plan for how they're going to develop security skills in each job function. While each role needs to understand fundamentals of secure development, privacy protection, and cloud infrastructure, additional job-specific training is needed. For example:

Product Owners	Mitigate risk in supporting the application. Safeguard data based on application, infrastructure, and operating environment.
Cloud Architects	Securely design applications deployed on cloud infrastructure. Analyze implementation options for core features. Analyze configuration options for architectural frameworks, API gateways, and microservices.
Developers	Need to know more about the environment and deployment but importantly need to know how to secure the code they write and what they need to know about security to write secure code.
Code Release Managers	Detect and mitigate insecure interfaces and APIs. Prevent common vulnerabilities. Recognize insufficient identity controls and insecure or out-of-date dependencies.

Site Reliability Engineers (SREs)	Understand how adverse events such as denial-of-service (DoS) attacks affect availability. Implement application whitelisting and apply least privileged access to data.
Automation Engineers	Leverage automation without compromising security. Conduct vulnerability assessments.
Operations	Need to script things and understand what they are deploying and how it interacts with other components.

In all cases, the ideal scenarios are when yellow teams are educated about red attack tactics and work hand in hand with blue teams to learn how to defend against those attacks. Yellow teams need to be *involved* in order to secure any organization, application, or IT system.

Enabling Yellow Teams with a Security Mindset

For build teams, you need to offer training sessions and ethical hacking courses, as these are generally not offered in universities. Teaching developers how attackers break into applications, networks, and infrastructure is an eye-opening experience and frequently inspires the team to incorporate security as part of its quality initiatives. Teach them how to mitigate attacks with good design and coding practices for a proactive defense. It works wonderfully.

When yellow teams work closely with red and blue teams, the organization becomes committed to mixing skills between builders, breakers, and defenders. This makes both the IT system being built more secure and the organization more secure. This is also the precursor to the secondary colored teams I discuss in the next chapter (purple, orange, and green).

A Quick Word on Security Champions

It's not practical to make everyone on build teams a security expert. Many companies have used the concept of *security champions* to embed security into a build team. This is a senior contributor who can work with and speak to the rest of the build team in familiar terminology. These security champions have credibility with build teams because they're "one of their own" as opposed to a blue teamer trying to force security into an established build process.

Gartner published a report called "3 Steps to Integrate Security into DevOps" wherein they suggest the implementation of a belt system, similar to martial arts (see Figure 3.3).

Security champions (or *coaches*, as Gartner calls them) start with an entry-level security belt and progress to the next phase after they've completed certain training requirements and on-the-job activities related to security.

These practitioners are knowledgeable about engineering and serve as security mentors to their teammates. These guardians of high-quality software and IT systems serve to do the following:

- Determine when to engage the security team
- Be the single point of contact in their build group
- Define goals and responsibilities related to security
- Conduct and/or verify security reviews
- Create and promote "best practices" across the build team
- Raise issues for risks in existing and new software/IT systems
- Build threat models for new features to analyze risks prior to creating those features

Sample Security Coach Advancement Program

Level	Guideline Training Prerequisites	Advancement and Improvement	Application Security Task to Maintain Level
Blue Belt	• Completed **10** training courses • Basic secure coding training including OWASP Top 10	• Complete in 3 CTFs and average score of **500** • **10** code sprints with no high-severity vulnerabilities	• Assist in gathering security testing requirements for applications relevant to their domain
Purple Belt	• Completed **15** training courses • Advanced training on specific vulnerability types, security architecture and/or language specifics	• Complete in 5 CTFs and average score of **1,000** • **25** code sprints with no high-severity vulnerabilities	• Provide feedback into secure coding practices and annual reviews • Assist with AST remediation activity for applications relevant to their domain
Brown Belt	• Completed **20** training courses	• Complete in 5 CTFs and place in **top 10** • **50** code sprints with no high-severity vulnerabilities	• Assist with drafting secure coding practices • Perform AST remediation activity independently for applications relevant to their domain
Black Belt	• Completed **25** training courses • Industry certification or presented on topics related to secure coding or design	• Train others • Create improved practices	• Serve as authors or custodians for secure coding practices in their domain • Generate threat models for applications relevant to their domain • Assist in bug triaging for reported incidents

Figure 3.3   Creating security champions

Key Functions of the Yellow Team

Here are the key functions of yellow teams in the NICE Securely Provision (SP) categories:

- **Security assessment and testing:** Yellow teams perform comprehensive security assessments and testing activities on an organization's systems, applications, and infrastructure. They simulate cyberattacks and vulnerabilities to identify weaknesses in the early stages of system development.

- **Policy and compliance evaluation:** Yellow teams review and evaluate an organization's security policies and compliance

Primary Colors: Foundational Cybersecurity Work Roles

measures in the context of SP. They ensure that security standards and best practices are integrated into the design and provisioning of systems.

- **Security integration:** Yellow teams work closely with system developers, architects, and engineers to integrate security requirements into the development and provisioning processes. They ensure that security is not an afterthought but a core consideration from the outset.

- **Threat modeling:** Yellow teams engage in threat modeling exercises, identifying potential threats and vulnerabilities specific to the systems and applications being provisioned. This proactive approach helps prevent security gaps.

- **Education and training:** Yellow teams play a critical role in educating development and provisioning teams about security best practices, ensuring that security is a shared responsibility throughout the organization.

- **Incident response planning:** In collaboration with blue teams, yellow teams help develop incident response plans that address potential security incidents and breaches during the provisioning phase. This proactive planning minimizes the impact of security incidents.

Benefits of a Security-Minded Yellow Team

The integration of yellow teams into the secure culture of an organization offers several benefits.

- **Early detection of vulnerabilities:** Yellow teams help identify and mitigate security vulnerabilities at the earliest stages of system development and provisioning, reducing the risk of costly security incidents later in the life cycle.

- **Enhanced security posture:** By focusing on security from the outset, yellow teams help organizations establish a strong foundation for their cybersecurity efforts, improving their overall security posture.

- **Cost savings:** Identifying and addressing security issues early in the development process is more cost-effective than addressing them after systems are in production. Yellow teams contribute to cost savings by preventing security incidents.

- **Compliance and risk mitigation:** Yellow teams assist organizations in complying with cybersecurity regulations and standards, reducing the risk of noncompliance and associated penalties.

- **Security awareness:** Through education and training, yellow teams raise security awareness among development and provisioning teams, fostering a culture of security in the organization.

Yellow Team Roles That Align with NICE

I've covered many job titles that make up the yellow team. Now let's look at some of the NICE work roles in the context of the yellow team builders, with appropriate translations juxtaposed to each work role. There are 10 to 12 work roles I can argue belong squarely in the yellow slice. Most fall into the Securely Provision category, but some from Operate and Maintain are listed here as well. Here are some of the more commonly found work roles that align with the yellow team:

- **Systems requirements planners (SP):** Consult with customers, legal, compliance, and other organizational leaders to gather and evaluate functional requirements and translate these requirements into technical solutions. Provide guidance to customers about applicability of information systems to meet business needs.

- **Enterprise architects (SP):** Conceptualize, design, procure, and/or build secure IT systems. Translate technology and environmental requirements, for example, laws and regulations, into system and security designs and processes. Develop IT rules and requirements that describe baseline and target architectures.

- **Software developers (SP):** Develop and write/code new (or modify existing) computer applications, software, or specialized utility programs following software assurance best practices, as well as requirements and design specifications.

- **System testing and evaluation specialists (SP):** Develop and conduct tests of IT systems to evaluate compliance with specifications and requirements. Apply principles and methods for cost-effective planning, evaluating, verifying, and validating technical, functional, performance, and security characteristics of IT systems. Plan, prepare, and execute tests to evaluate desired results against specifications and requirements as well as analyze and report test results.

- **Database administrators (OM):** Develop and administer databases and/or data management systems that allow for the secure storage, query, protection, and utilization of data.

- **Network operations specialists (OM):** Install, deploy, configure, test, operate, maintain, and manage software applications and the networks on which they reside, including firewalls, hubs, bridges, switches, multiplexers, routers, cables, proxy servers, and so on, that permit the sharing and transmission of information to support the security IT systems.

Follow the Yellow Brick Road to Security

Yellow teams, while not explicitly defined within the NICE Framework, offer a valuable approach to enhancing cybersecurity within the Securely Provision categories, better known as *development teams*. These teams play a crucial role in building the systems that run the enterprise; however, they also should play a critical role in identifying vulnerabilities, integrating security into development processes, and promoting a proactive approach to cybersecurity throughout the entire product/development organization. By combining elements of both offensive and defensive practices into their development efforts, yellow teams help organizations build secure foundations for their systems and applications, ultimately reducing risks and strengthening overall security posture. As cybersecurity continues to evolve, the concept of security-empowered yellow teams holds promise in fostering a holistic and proactive approach to cybersecurity within all organizations.

Summary

The primary colors of the cybersecurity color wheel comprise three-fourths of the major work roles focused on security as their core responsibility. I discuss the fourth (white teams) in Chapter 5; however, if you are thinking about careers in cybersecurity, chances are the work roles associated with red and blue teams come to mind first. After all, these are the breakers and defenders most people imagine when cybersecurity is brought to mind.

The third color discussed, yellow teams, are the builders who make the many technology systems that drive our world. Having these yellow teamers operate in a security vacuum does a disservice to their creative and quality abilities; worse, doing so enhances the risk of every system they construct. Therefore, it is of paramount importance to introduce yellow teams to the fundamental elements of red and blue teams. As discussed in the next chapter, the resulting secondary colors serve as a catalyst to supercharge an organization's cybersecurity posture—often without needing to hire more cybersecurity professionals.

Red, blue, and yellow teams are well represented in the NICE Framework. As you will soon learn, the secondary colors are not, despite their importance in the evolution of cybersecurity in the modern digital enterprise.

Chapter 4

Secondary Colors: Interdisciplinary Cybersecurity Work Roles

This chapter looks at the secondary color groups, which represent the interdisciplinary cybersecurity work roles you get when mixing two of the primary colors together. In this chapter, you learn new roles that are specific to the cybersecurity industry, such as purple teams; and you learn the value of adding security skills to the roles in the yellow/builder category.

Creating green and orange teams creates value for the individuals in those roles, as they achieve new capabilities and differentiate themselves from former peers who do not possess such skills. Green and orange teams also add significant value to the organization. As you will see in some of the case studies in Chapter 8, when nonsecurity work roles are exposed to and educated on security tasks, they start asking different questions considering the security implications of the activities they may have otherwise taken for granted or simply accepted without question.

Purple: The Evolution of Cyber Innovation

Purple is the most commonly known and referred to secondary color in cybersecurity. The objective is to combine the primary capabilities of offensive tactics (red) and defensive tactics (blue) into a blended powerhouse of knowledge and capability. The power of "purple teaming" is all about strengthening cyber defense through collaboration. The origins of this color slice can be found in the military arena of war gaming. My youth and appetite for cybersecurity was colored by a popular movie—1983's *War Games*. It's about a teenage hacker who accidentally encounters a NORAD supercomputer known as WOPR (War Operation Plan Response). WOPR was built to continuously run nuclear war simulations and learn to improve itself over time; it was built by a fictional early artificial intelligence (AI) researcher. I write about some of the cybersecurity benefits and risks of artificial intelligence in Chapter 6. In the movie, the teenage hacker breaks into the system by reverse-engineering the master password after doing some elementary reconnaissance on WOPR's builder. I could write plenty about the power and utility of two-factor authentication, but for now, suffice it to say that this fundamental "best practice" is still not nearly as pervasive as it should be 50 years after *War Games* hit theaters.

The attack landscape is constantly evolving in cybersecurity; the battle between attackers and defenders is relentless. It is, for all intents and purposes, a digital arms race. To stay ahead of sophisticated threats and adapt to emerging attack vectors, organizations are embracing innovative approaches like purple teaming.

As mentioned, the purple slice has gained prominence in recent years. This concept involves collaborative efforts between the traditional red team (offensive) and blue team (defensive) roles with the ultimate goal being to enhance cyber defense strategies. Purple is the one secondary color that now has explicit job titles and work roles associated with it—including the color in the job title even! Before discussing jobs that are directly purple as well as the red and blue jobs that are commonly blended, let me delve a bit more deeply into the concept of purple teaming, its significance in bolstering cyber resilience, and how it contributes to a more effective and proactive cybersecurity posture.

Understanding Purple Teaming

Purple teaming can be thought of as a fusion of the strengths of the red and blue teams, working in unison to create a more comprehensive and robust defense strategy. Traditionally, red teams simulate cyberattacks to identify vulnerabilities and weaknesses in an organization's systems, while blue teams focus on defending against these attacks and maintaining security. Purple teaming bridges the gap between these two roles, fostering collaboration, information sharing, and real-time learning.

In a purple teaming scenario, members from both teams come together to jointly simulate and respond to various attack scenarios. These "joint ops" not only provide an opportunity to test the effectiveness of existing security measures but also encourage knowledge exchange, enabling defenders to understand attackers' tactics, techniques, and procedures (TTPs). The ultimate goal is to assess and improve an organization's overall cyber defense strategy by enhancing detection, response, and mitigation capabilities. The more creative the red team is in its attacks, the more resilient it forces the blue team to be in its defenses. The act of purple teaming has now created jobs dedicated to the development of purple team activities in an organization's information security and risk management organizations. Cybersecurity vendors have also created products, training, and service lines of business dedicated to delivering purple team solutions or helping organizations develop purple team activities internally. It's a brilliant development in our industry.

There are seven main areas where purple teaming provides important value in cyber defense initiatives, discussed in the following sections.

Improved Incident Response

When red and blue teams work together in purple teaming exercises, they gain insights into how threats are executed, detected, and countered. This experience is invaluable in refining incident response processes, as defenders become better equipped to identify, isolate, and mitigate threats in real time. Much has been written about advanced persistent threats (APTs); however, to me, the element of APTs that has the highest potential for serious and long-term damage to an organization is the "persistent" element. Many different forms of malware exist on an organization's network for weeks or months prior to discovery. During this persistent yet undiscovered phase, the malware is often conducting reconnaissance to find vulnerable assets on which it can release its payload.

Preparing for such situations is critical to an organization's ability to mitigate damage and respond to malware detection (as an example). These simulations can be conducted using tools like a *cyber range* that can reasonably mimic an organization's infrastructure in a segmented environment. A malicious payload can be released on such an isolated (and virtual) network where resilience of the infrastructure can be measured, as can the responses taken by the team upon discovery. In these simulations, a red teamer will typically develop a script that uses known malware, whereas blue teamers emulate the defenses deployed on the enterprise network. Once the attack is released, automated responses will be triggered (ideally) and critical assets checked for integrity and availability.

Cyber ranges are valuable tools in the cybersecurity arsenal and are extremely rich learning environments. A cyber range mimics an actual IT deployment and can be used for offensive (red team) or defensive (blue team) exercises. Consider it like a gaming environment ... a safe sandbox in which you can try different things without the worry of creating damage. It's like a scrimmage game in sports, where you can practice against a real opponent, but the results don't count in any standings or contest. You can also think about cyber ranges as the cybersecurity equivalent of a flight simulator for airline pilots. Some cyber ranges mimic your own IT environment and allow you to test the defenses you've built; other ranges are intentionally vulnerable IT environments that let you try your penetration testing or other "attack" techniques.

Maximized ROI on Security Investments

By identifying weaknesses and gaps in existing security measures, purple teaming allows organizations to allocate resources effectively. Instead of investing in technologies that may not align with actual threats, organizations can focus on solutions that directly address their vulnerabilities. These simulation exercises mentioned are particularly valuable tools when used specifically for this purpose. Ideally, organizations can conduct purple team exercises during the evaluation or pilot phase of a particular defense technology, tactic, or procedure to assess its effectiveness *in situ* with the infrastructure used to run the enterprise.

Realistic Testing and Training

Red teaming emulates real-world attack scenarios, offering a more accurate representation of potential threats. When blue teams are trained on these attacks before they occur (either in simulation or in reality), they are better equipped to build defenses to thwart the attack and mitigate damage. This education process, combined with the attack emulation activities, yields some of the highest fidelity testing possible. Likewise, prior to an attack simulation exercise, red teams can be trained on the defenses currently in place. This equips them with knowledge they can use to try to evade, disable, or trick these defenses. Clever attackers will mask malicious intent behind behavior or traffic that appears legitimate so as to not trip intrusion prevention systems (IPSs) or intrusion detection systems (IDSs).

This practical approach allows organizations to identify vulnerabilities that might go unnoticed in traditional testing methods. It's precisely the same practice you'll read about when reading about the orange team process. The "defenders" on orange teams are typically software/IT testers (aka quality assurance professionals). Those test/QA staff are members of the yellow team. Teaching them red team tactics creates the orange slice. But more on that later.

Regardless of whether this realistic testing and training is done as part of purple or orange team exercises, the main benefit is the same: by exposing weaknesses via attack tactics, defenders can gain insights into their security posture and can proactively address vulnerabilities before malicious actors exploit them in production.

Enhanced Collaboration

Collaboration is at the core of purple teaming. It encourages communication and shared knowledge between red and blue teams, fostering a greater understanding of each other's perspectives. While the information sharing often happens under the guise of a technical attack simulation, the real valuable learning comes from understanding the tactics and procedures used (not necessarily the technology). This is important because, just as there are many ways to compromise a particular asset, there are also numerous ways in which to defend it. Rather than trying to construct an uber defense coalition of technology-specific defenses, purple teaming enables the generation of resilient fortifications specific to the *technique* used. This allows teams to defend against a multitude of attacks that may use different technologies applied using the same or similar tactic. This collaboration leads to improved incident response procedures, better detection techniques, and more effective mitigation strategies.

Adaptive Defense Strategies

We have established that cyber attackers are constantly evolving their tactics. Defenders need to be equally adaptive so as to impede these evolving dangers. Purple teaming helps defenders keep pace by exposing them to the latest attack techniques and trends, forcing an "adapt or peril" imperative that may otherwise not exist, due to either hubris or ignorance. This exposure enables organizations to both revise and fine-tune their defense strategies to stay ahead of (or at least maintain pace with) emerging threats. Purple teaming yields adaptive defense strategies, but only to those organizations willing to also adapt its culture, which leads me to...

Cultural Transformation

Purple teaming is intended to encourage a shift in organizational culture toward a proactive and collaborative mindset. The concept is to break down silos between "attack" and "defend" teams and promote knowledge sharing. This is not a forgone conclusion when an organization commits itself to adopt purple teaming activities. Cultural transformation almost always requires executive buy-in. Without it, the organization is forced to either make trade-offs between purple teaming and other cybersecurity spend (both budget and staff); or worse, the organization decides to adopt this strategy only after a catastrophic event plunges it into emergency incident response.

Purple teaming can be a highly effective tactic to foster the very sense of collective responsibility for cybersecurity needed to make it successful.

Risk Reduction

Ultimately, purple teaming leads to a reduction in overall cyber risk. This is the nirvana of all cybersecurity professionals and, increasingly, a global strategic initiative for executives and boards in all industries. A main objective of purple teaming is to identify vulnerabilities and weaknesses before they are exploited to help organizations minimize the potential impact of breaches and attacks. This highly valuable risk reduction can be realized only when an organization has made the necessary commitments to cultural change, budgets, communication, education, and governance that enable successful purple team endeavors.

Dancing in the Purple Rain

If purple teaming sounds like an interesting career option for you, whether you're an existing cybersecurity professional or keen to become one, you are not alone. It is an exciting and emerging field in our industry. Information security and IT executives, as well as leaders in human resources, can look to purple teaming for a rich field of professional development opportunities. It's a great way to retain red and blue team members who are highly sought after. If you commit to the cultural and budgetary training necessary to enable purple team activities, you will make your organization more attractive to the very talent that is in short supply in our industry. It will also provide you a platform with which to revisit existing job descriptions, career paths, and work roles in your organization. You can further develop yourself and your organization at the same time you offer professional development opportunities to staff members.

You may find you want to create new positions, seek new sources of employee education, or start to expose nonsecurity professionals to the world of cyber as a way to enhance your enterprise security hygiene.

> While the NICE Framework does not explicitly have roles labeled as "purple teaming," there are work roles that encompass a combination of offensive and defensive skills, which align with the collaborative spirit of purple teaming. As mentioned, a very promising (and useful) trend I noticed starting in early 2023 is that some jobs are now including the term *purple team* in the title and job description itself. The concept of a position focused on blending tactics, facilitating education, and information sharing—and otherwise assisting red and blue teams to do their respective jobs better—is a fascinating and most welcomed development in the cybersecurity industry.

Given the fact that purple teaming involves the collaboration and coordination between red teams (offensive) and blue teams (defensive) to enhance overall cybersecurity strategies, let's explore some of the work roles that share attributes with purple team activities. I've adapted some NICE work roles to better align with actual job functions of purple teamers since none exists in the framework itself.

Cybersecurity Engineer

This work role can include elements of cyber operator, cyber ops planner, and cybersecurity engineers, and professionals who design and implement security solutions, considering both offensive and defensive strategies. They ensure that security measures are effective and aligned with the organization's overall cybersecurity goals.

Cybersecurity Analyst

Included here are NICE work roles titled cyber defense/forensics analyst, cyber network operations specialist, and systems security analyst. Cybersecurity analysts work to identify vulnerabilities, analyze security incidents, and develop strategies to mitigate risks. The role involves elements of both offensive and defensive techniques to protect systems and data. Cyber analysts analyze network traffic, investigate incidents, and recommend strategies to protect against threats. Their role combines elements of the red and blue teams to enhance overall cybersecurity.

Information Systems Security Manager

Information systems security managers (ISSMs) oversee the security of information systems, which involves collaborating with the red and blue teams to ensure security policies are in place, managing security incidents, and implementing holistic cybersecurity strategies.

Cyber Operations Planner/Operator

CyOps professionals develop detailed intelligence plans to satisfy cyber operations requirements. They collaborate with the red and blue team planners to identify, validate, and levy requirements for data collection and analysis of purple teaming exercises. They participate in targeting selection, validation, synchronization, and execution of cyber actions, synchronizing intelligence activities to support organization objectives in cyberspace. Their work involves understanding both offensive and defensive tactics to ensure an effective incident response.

Security Control Assessor

Security control assessors evaluate security controls and measures to ensure compliance and effectiveness. They collaborate with different teams to ensure that security measures align with both offensive and defensive strategies. Security control assessors also conduct independent comprehensive assessments of the management, operational, and technical security controls deployed during purple teaming to determine the overall effectiveness of those controls.

Mission Assessment Specialist/Vulnerability Assessment Analyst

These security engineers, as they are typically called in organizations that haven't adopted the NICE Framework, spend their time designing and implementing security solutions that encompass both red and blue approaches. They work to find weak spots in the IT infrastructure, prevent unauthorized access, monitor for anomalies, and respond to security incidents. The mission-focused work roles develop assessment plans and measures of performance and effectiveness. They conduct strategic and operational effectiveness assessments, as required, for cyber events. They assist in determining whether systems performed as expected and provide input to determine operational effectiveness.

Incident Responder

Incident responders are responsible for detecting and responding to cybersecurity incidents. Their collaboration with red and blue teams ensures effective incident analysis, containment, and recovery. The preparation done for incident response can be fine-tuned during purple team exercises and is invaluable for validating security controls. One NICE work role I place in this category is communications security (COMSEC) manager. This role needs the skill to determine how a security system should work (including its resilience and dependability capabilities) and how changes in conditions, operations, or environment (think attack, data breach, or inappropriate privacy/ information disclosure, i.e., "incident") affect these outcomes.

71

Threat Hunter

Threat hunters proactively search for signs of malicious activity and potential threats in an organization's systems. Their work involves a combination of understanding attack tactics and employing defensive strategies. The closest work role in the NICE Framework is the threat/warning analyst. This job develops cyber indicators to maintain awareness of the status of the highly dynamic IT environments in most cyber operations. Threat/warning analysts collect, process, analyze, and disseminate cyber threat assessments, including purple team activities.

Cybersecurity Architect/Consultant

Cybersecurity architects are referred to as enterprise architects in the NICE Framework. This work role is rapidly evolving from a *blue-dominated* job to a *green-dominated* job. Historically, a cybersecurity architect was focused only on constructing defenses. This is why NICE placed the enterprise architect work role in the category of *Securely Provision* (a "blue" function) and the specialty area of *Systems Architecture* (a "yellow" function). Combining the two yields a "green" function. Consider how NICE describes what they call enterprise architect:

> Develop and maintain business, systems, and information processes to support enterprise cybersecurity mission needs. Develop information technology (IT) rules and requirements that describe secure baseline and target architectures.

This role is all about providing expert advice and guidance on cybersecurity strategies, drawing from mainly defensive knowledge to recommend comprehensive solutions that are to be built. It's a green job. In the context of purple teaming, cybersecurity and enterprise architects are deeply invested observers of any war gaming or threat modeling that occurs. After all, it is their design getting attacked; they'll want to know how well the architecture withstood the barrage and make necessary changes where their defenses failed.

Industry Example of Purple Team Jobs

Like I have done with other color slices, let me offer some insight into actual job titles I've seen at organizations that span the tech, manufacturing, retail, finance, and government sectors. The jobs and summary descriptions are taken directly from companies including Meta, Toyota, Home Depot, Wells Fargo, and the Washington DC Metro. Note how many use terms such as *collaborate, diverse, communicate, culture,* and *effectiveness.*

- **Offensive security engineer, purple team:** Deliver technical attack expertise for the purple team initiatives. This individual should have extensive experience across the attack life cycle and a demonstrated capacity to lead, design, and execute collaborative efforts with partners to test the effectiveness of defenses in place for a target.

- **Purple team engineer (offensive and defensive):** You are a specialist who knows how to exploit discovered flaws and remediate them; develop/implement automated systems; run red team simulation exercises; and assess incident response effectiveness. You will be part of a very diverse team that is highly collaborative, with the ability to build relationships with colleagues from different cultures throughout the organization.

- **Cybersecurity analyst III/purple:** Develop comprehensive reports and presentations for both technical and executive audiences; effectively communicate findings and strategy;

facilitate recommendations to correct vulnerabilities; safely utilize attacker tools, tactics, and procedures.

- **Purple team lead:** Provide assurance on cyber detection and response capabilities, train network defenders, and help to increase the security posture of the enterprise through providing subject-matter expertise during cyber incidents.

- **Lead cybersecurity research consultant, purple team:** Perform tactical cyberattack evaluation, exploit testing and analysis, cyber intelligence, and red or purple teaming. Regularly collaborate with multiple teams. Help enable a strong risk mitigation and compliance-driven culture.

- **Senior infosec incident response specialist, purple team:** Conduct noncomplex strategic assessments on systems and networks to determine potential cyber threat opportunities. Analyze noncomplex events and anomalies in accordance with IT security directives, including initiating, responding, and reporting discovered events.

- **Red team/purple team cybersecurity engineer:** Organize and conduct goal-based red team exercises, coordinate external red team engagements, collaborate with the blue team to conduct ongoing purple team exercises based on evolving threats and identify control gaps, and produce high-quality, actionable reporting and recommendations on those activities.

- **Technical threat manager:** Plan and execute all purple teaming engagements and attack simulations, and manage deception technology. Work closely with other teams in the cybersecurity group to push the boundaries of technology in a fast-paced and dynamic environment. In addition to technical skills, the technical threat manager requires great communication skills and the ability to work collaboratively.

The Cybersecurity Future Is Purple

While the NICE Framework roles may not be explicitly labeled as "purple teaming," many roles involve a blend of offensive and defensive skills, making them essential contributors to a collaborative approach that aligns with the spirit of purple teaming. The industry is ahead of NICE in this instance and already incorporating purple team roles, titles, and tasks into jobs that are in high demand. You may have observed that many purple team job functions begin with red team attacks and offensive measures; therefore, if you are keen or have a penchant for breaking, hacking, and proactive testing, you could find a very lucrative career in *either* red team or purple team roles. In many ways, purple teaming is the next evolutionary wave of cybersecurity. It builds on one of the core pillars of security (breaking), but bleeds into the uber-important defending pillar, making purple people, if you will, extremely valuable to their organizations.

Leaders and other executives would be wise to proactively invest in existing staff to develop purple team talent or stand up dedicated purple teams. In an age where cyber threats are becoming increasingly sophisticated, a proactive and collaborative approach to cybersecurity is paramount. Purple teaming bridges the gap between offense and defense, bringing together the red and blue teams to work in harmony. If you can't create these teams from scratch, which admittedly is a difficult thing to do, look to your existing staff to provide professional development opportunities and career pathing you may not have previously considered. It is an easy way to retain the valuable talent that is likely to leave for more fertile, interesting work elsewhere. As with all of the secondary colors, purple teaming is more about developing talent and adding skills to your current workforce. It provides an opportunity to revisit job descriptions, learning journeys, and career construct retention pathways for your staff. This becomes even more relevant in the coming two colors—orange and green—as their

Secondary Colors: Interdisciplinary Cybersecurity Work Roles

primary jobs are something *other* than security. Strategically, organizations that embrace purple teaming are better positioned to withstand and mitigate the challenges posed by emerging threats.

Through realistic testing, enhanced collaboration, improved incident response, adaptive defense strategies, and a transformed organizational culture, purple teaming strengthens cyber defense strategies and contributes to a more resilient cybersecurity posture. Purple, born from the fusion of red and blue, symbolizes the innovative and collaborative aspects of the skills and tasks in a number of different work roles in the NICE Framework. These roles drive technological advancements, explore emerging trends, and pioneer new solutions to combat evolving cyber threats. Work roles such as research scientist and cybersecurity architect are primed to emerge as strategically vital elements of a cybersecurity strategy and help to shape the future of cybersecurity.

Orange and Green: Injecting the Builders with a Security Mindset

In Chapter 3, I introduce the concept of yellow teams using the analogy of building a house. There I discuss how the builders are responsible for these five key phases of development:

- Definition
- Design
- Construction
- Testing
- Deployment and maintenance

For the orange and green secondary colors, I'm going to expand on that a bit and borrow from the world of software development to discuss the job functions and career paths these two underrecognized colors provide. I write more about software security specifically and the plethora of opportunities it provides in Chapter 6. Everything that I discuss in the next two sections can apply equally to cloud, web, IoT, mobile, network, and other types of IT systems "development." I use the software realm as the lens from which to deliver the prose about these palette splotches because, regardless of which deployment environment you end up considering, software will undoubtedly be a relevant factor because of its ubiquitous and omnipresent nature in all things IT.

The orange and green slices of the cybersecurity color wheel have the fewest work roles defined in the NICE Framework; in fact, I argue there are exactly zero. Unlike purple, which has evolved from the two core colors of cybersecurity (red and blue), these two secondary colors have their common base in yellow—the builders who make all of the IT systems that drive our digital world. I'll take them one at a time, and instead of following the NICE Framework, I follow the seven major phases of every yellow team (see Figure 4.1):

- Plan/Define
- Design/Code
- Build/Develop
- Test/Validate
- Release/Package
- Deploy/Adopt
- Monitor/Observe

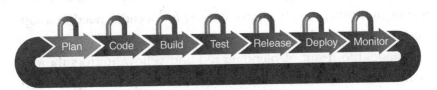

Figure 4.1 The seven phases of system development

You will see me use the word *pairs* in each of the seven phases interchangeably; in particular, I favor one word over the other when it applies (or implies) more than one of the two core colors of cyber-security (red and blue).

Orange: The Hulk's Approach to SysDev

In keeping with my fiction- and color-themed movie references, I ironically summon the green Hulk character when discussing the value of the orange slice of the cybersecurity color wheel. The Hulk is an aggressive brute with an anger management issue. He means well; after all, he's one of the Marvel Avengers. He's one of the "good guys," but his approach is a bit rough. Ultimately, the Hulk gets the job done—especially when working in concert with his less aggressive peers. What the Hulk does to buildings and "bad guys" is what I suggest we need to do to the various cloud, web, IoT, mobile, network, and other types of IT systems we build with our yellow teams.

NICE refers to the yellow slice as Securely Provision (SP), but the work roles it defines there have a lot to be desired. *Authorizing official/designating representative*? I can honestly say I've never seen that job title in my 20+ years in the IT security field. *Systems requirements planner* and *research and development specialist* get a little bit closer to common yellow team job titles that exist in the industry, but they still miss the mark. Regardless, what I want to drive home about the orange and green slices is more about the on-the-job activities that should be *added* to *existing* work roles. product managers, cloud architects, test engineers, DevOps managers, database administrators, and other jobs that have existed for decades need to adopt some Hulkian attitudes as part of their daily functions.

Orange, the result of blending red and yellow, mirrors the collaborative nature of builders and breakers. Orange teaming is a very new concept in cybersecurity. It focuses on collaborative exercises between red teams and yellow teams to improve an organization's security posture. The basic concept is to teach attack techniques to development teams: *The Hulk's Approach to SysDev*.

As previously mentioned, the NICE Framework does not have any specific roles labeled as "orange teaming," but the concept aligns with roles that involve both offensive and provisioning skills. In the following sections, I examine the seven phases of IT system development shown in Figure 4.1. For each phase, I use at least one common job title and its main job function; I then introduce activities that the job should consider adopting to color its original yellow tint more orange.

Plan/Define

This phase is the realm of the product manager, program manager, business analyst, product owner, requirements manager, and the like. The main purpose of this work role is to define the system to be built; that is, what are the requirements? The specification? The elements needed to execute the business objective and comply with compliance, legal, and other mandates in the process? Common deliverables from this function are things like use cases, spec docs (functional, performance, etc.), and the like.

When building a house, you might plan for a four-bedroom Colonial style with two bathrooms. A performance requirement might be suitable capacity and plumbing (water flow) for a family of five. When building an IT system, you might plan for an e-commerce application style with shopping cart functionality. A performance requirement might be the ability to process 500 orders per hour. Typically, the yellow team activity stops here, so let's invoke our inner Hulk and imagine an attack on the e-commerce system. You could use this to augment the use case and requirement activity. For example, the performance requirement might change to be able to process 500 orders per hour while simultaneously withstanding a denial-of-service (DoS) attack that's flooding the web application with 100 login attempts per second.

That is how to turn a yellow business analyst into an orange business analyst. Would you be more valuable to your organization if you knew how to augment your requirements specs with these offensive use/abuse cases? As a development team lead or IT executive, wouldn't you want your product owners to be able to add this additional value early in the system/software development lifecycle (SDLC) rather than waiting for the security team to run this test case (which will probably happen well into the deployment phase)? If you've read anything about the concept of "shifting security left" in the world of DevOps and IT systems development, this is it. In fact, it doesn't get any more shifted left than this.

> *Shift left* is an industry term used to describe the movement of security functions earlier in the IT system acquisition and/or development life cycle. Historically, security testing and reporting was a post-deployment phenomenon. Instantiating some of this work into the pre-deployment phases of define, design, acquire, build, and test is referred to as *shifting security left*. The theory is if we incorporate security considerations early, we are less likely to propagate problems from a flawed base and less likely to encounter vulnerabilities that are difficult and expensive to fix later in the SDLC.

Need some inspiration for attacks to imagine? I refer you to the excellently documented and completely free resource of the MITRE ATT&CK Framework (see `https://attack.mitre.org`). Alternatively, you can seek one of many qualified training partners to help educate your yellow build teams on security, in this case, red offensive tactics.

Design/Code

We move to the world of architects now. These are the software, cloud, IoT, IT, and other system designers that build our blueprints. Note the use of the word *code* here does not indicate software development, programming, or coding per se—that is more directly relevant in the build/develop phase discussed next. Many IT architects do write software code and/or come from a coding background; however, their primary function is to choose the most appropriate components to meet the requirements specified in the planning phase. The design elements include the selection of technologies and diagramming of relationships that define the system, the business transactions it will process, and the users it will support.

An architect designing a house will choose the trusses, beams, room shapes and size, and other structures that define what is to be built. Building architects consider safety when designing homes. They consider the effect of "attacks" such as hurricanes, heavy snow loads on the roof, and other negative events to ensure the house is resilient and able to resist those occurrences. That red teaming activity is baked into every structural architect's world from the earliest days of their schooling; they are orange teamers by default. Not so in the IT world. It is incumbent upon the industry to introduce analogous red teaming activity to software, cloud, and IT system architects to turn them from yellow to orange. We will make their lives easier if we specify attack scenarios during the use-case development in the planning phase.

Let's continue building on the previous use case regarding performance, a functional spec that we augmented with a red team attack: *process 500 orders per hour while simultaneously withstanding a DoS attack that's flooding the web application with 100 login attempts per second.*

This would force the architect to consider the DoS attack (akin to a roof collapsing under heavy snow load) and learn about or simulate it if they don't already know how that threat would impact the design. After the orange team exercise, they would look to choose a design element that helps them still meet the functional requirement under that level of duress. It might trigger, as an example, a research activity that lands on the selection of a cloud service provider's authentication service that allows for login monitoring and throttling of login attempts aimed specifically to thwart DoS attacks. If the architect hadn't acted (even mentally) as an attacker during the design phase, the result might end up one that is susceptible to common attacks like DoS.

Build/Develop

A critically important phase in SDLC, in build/develop you will find job titles such as software engineer, system developer, programmer, and most commonly developer. These yellow teamers are the implementers. They take the planning requirements and any architectural constraints and build the IT system. The word *build* is an overloaded term because it includes the process of assembling from various open-source, commercial, off-the-shelf, and custom-built elements of software code, hardware, and third-party services.

Training developers on red team tactics is one of the most valuable and highly leverageable activities an organization can conduct. Most research and development (R&D) teams seldom imagine that their system will be misused, either maliciously or unintentionally. Of course, this happens all the time. Because development teams typically don't consider misuse, they consequently do not code defensively. In the IT world, making orange build teams is easy in concept, but vast in scope. This group tends to be the most numerous and the technology stacks they use are both very diverse and constantly changing. The result is a significant challenge for those tasks with educating them on attack techniques. That person or group needs to cover, as best as possible, the technologies used when creating IT systems and software applications. The best place to start, as usual, is with the fundamentals.

Start by teaching those who write software code and build the IT systems that run your enterprise the most common attacks for each major deployment platform. The Open Web Application Security Project, also known as OWASP (www.owasp.org), has some excellent free resources on common threats to web, mobile, cloud, IoT, and API platforms. The "Top 10" lists for each of those is a great place to start. The Top 10 lists represent a broad consensus about the most critical security risks. Every risk listed has example attack scenarios that can be used to exploit the weaknesses commonly found in each risk category. For example, the OWASP Top 10 Web Application Security Risks for 2021, the latest version as of the writing of this book, has "Broken Access Controls" as #1.

To continue with the house analogy, the house was designed to have a front door, but let's say the blueprint didn't specify that the door must have a lock. A development team following the plan and designing to the minimum requirements (to finish as quickly as possible) might use an interior door with no lock as the front door... after all, this meets the functional spec. But if that build team is aware of a possible "broken access control" attack, where, in this instance, anyone can enter the home even without possessing a key to unlock the front door, they might have built the door to include a lock (or more likely buy a pre-assembled door with lock from the parts store). This is the same thing that happens with IT systems. Let's say your e-commerce application allows any user to access past orders without providing any kind of identification. They might discover customer addresses, payment info, or other sensitive data because "the front door is unlocked."

A more poignant and frequently implemented scenario is that basic authentication is required, but it's merely a simple username and password combination. That username/password combination

Secondary Colors: Interdisciplinary Cybersecurity Work Roles

is then passed to the database in clear text; that is, the application uses unverified data in a SQL call to access account information—a reasonable and fast process. If the development team doesn't understand the basic attack that breaks this rudimentary authentication, the e-commerce site would allow an attacker to simply modify the browser's parameter that displays the account to send whatever account number they want. If that account information is not correctly protected and verified, an attacker can access any user account on the system.

Test/Validate

This is my favorite color slice in the entire wheel. It's all about the offensive testing of IT systems during the build process. This is distinctly different than the penetration testing done by red teams, although they share a lot of similar characteristics. Both are trying to find security flaws by proactively attacking the as-built system. Work roles here—quality assurance (QA), quality engineering (QE), test engineer, et al.—conduct this testing before the system is pushed into production. Just like the phases before it, these team members often don't carry out red team actions because they aren't educated on the world of attack.

Back to the house you're building. Rather than just verifying that the hot and cold water function properly, the front door stays closed when shut, and so on, orange teamers during the test phase should be trying unanticipated scenarios, such as attempting to "kick down the front door." In the IT world, this is perhaps the easiest step to imagine turning from yellow to orange. The best way to get started is to read about any of the attack scenarios listed in the OWASP Top 10 list relevant to your system and give them a try. Alternatively, try to carry out some of the approaches in the well-documented MITRE ATT&CK Framework.

Release/Package

Few people anticipated the SolarWinds hack that came to light at the end of 2020. Exploitation of commercial software products was and is a common occurrence, but one of the more dastardly pieces that set the SolarWinds attack apart from others is that it infiltrated the build process of the SolarWinds Orion software product. This compromised a digitally signed Orion network monitoring component, opening a backdoor into the networks of thousands of government and enterprise customers. This supply chain attack was carried out during the packaging and release phase of the SDLC, causing SolarWinds to unknowingly send out Orion software updates with the hacked code. To learn more about the SolarWinds attack, see this November 2023 article from Tech Target: `www.techtarget.com/whatis/feature/SolarWinds-hack-explained-Everything-you-need-to-know/`.

Release engineers can learn attack techniques such as update hijacking, code signing injection, and open-source code compromising and then craft tests for their application before compiling and releasing it to production. The same access control flaw discussed in previous phases can be leveraged during the packaging phase to embed malicious code that gets assembled with the entire application, effectively hiding it until it's ready to release its payload. The Cybersecurity and Infrastructure Security Agency (CISA) released an excellent white paper titled "Defending Against Software Supply Chain Attacks" (see `www.cisa.gov/sites/default/files/publications/defending_against_software_supply_chain_attacks_508_1.pdf`) that is particularly useful to the orange release engineer team.

Deploy/Adopt

Once considered a purely operational and tactical phase, deployment and configuration security is now of paramount importance to IT systems. The titles here include IT engineer, cloud engineer,

Secondary Colors: Interdisciplinary Cybersecurity Work Roles

DevOps engineer, site reliability engineer, and system administrator, among others. Because so many IT systems rely on cloud services from cloud service providers (CSPs) like Amazon Web Services, Microsoft Azure, and Google Cloud, this phase has become a favorite attack point for hackers. Unlike the direct attacks on IT systems, these attacks favor the misconfiguration of the APIs, microservices, and other products used when deploying business applications to the cloud. Those applications can be vulnerable via improperly configured permissions on cloud services, unnecessary features that are left enabled by default (such as unnecessary ports), and incorrect security settings in application servers and frameworks (for example, ASP.NET).

These "operators" need to adopt common attack scenarios and utilize threat modeling to ensure their systems—and the environments in which they are deployed—are properly secured. A common attack scenario is inspecting deployed application servers, which are easily discoverable with simple scanning tools. These application servers typically come with sample apps. If these are not removed from the production server and have a known security flaw, attackers can use the vulnerability to compromise the entire server. And if one of those applications is your administrative console with default username and password combination(s) that weren't changed, an attacker logs in with default passwords and is free to carry out nefarious behavior. Release engineers should also carry out reconnaissance missions to determine if detailed error messages, for example, stack traces, are being displayed to system users. This can potentially expose sensitive information such as component versions that are known to be vulnerable.

Monitor/Observe

Once your IT system is live, the important role of monitoring commences. Operations engineers, system integrators, technical/systems analysts, and network administrators need to start watching for risks to system confidentiality, integrity, and availability (known as *the CIA triad* of security). Of course, those yellow teams can watch for system risks only if they are properly educated in the red team offensive attacks that will help turn themselves orange. It may surprise you to learn that *security logging and monitoring failures* have been one of the OWASP Top 10 web threats listed for many years.

This work role helps detect, escalate, and respond to anomalous behavior or aberrant patterns. Without logging and monitoring, it is significantly more difficult to detect problems like data breaches. Insufficient monitoring and detection prevents active incident response and is common when events that are easily auditable, such as failed login attempts and high-value transactions, are not recorded. A simple technique deployed here is the implementation of common attacks, such as listed in the MITRE ATT&CK Framework, coupled with observing the behavior of the system during and after the attack. Rather than simply monitoring for system availability and integrity, proactively test for inappropriate information disclosure, failure to record failed logins, and unexplained changes in system behavior. Don the red cap of an attacker and turn that yellow system monitor orange.

While there are no work roles from the NICE Framework explicitly labeled as "orange teaming," the job functions described here encompass a distinctly offensive skill, making them integral to security efforts that align with the spirit of orange teaming for "builders."

Green: It's Not That Easy Being Green

It's not easy bein' green
It seems you blend in With so many other ordinary things
And people tend to pass you over
Cause you're not standing out

Like flashy sparkles in the water
Or stars in the sky
    Kermit the Frog famously sang in the song
    Bein' Green

"It seems you blend in…and people tend to pass you over cause you're not standing out." Most people view that as a negative consequence; however, in the world of cybersecurity, it is precisely what you want. When you're a "builder" on a yellow team, you're typically focused on pushing the features of your latest development live. You want users to love it and the rewards that come with that. As you should. But to a malicious actor who wants to do harm to your precious creation, you want to be just like Kermit the Frog. Cool and friendly-like, not flashy. And just like the song, it could make you wonder why. But, why wonder when green will do just fine? It's beautiful, and it's all you need to be.

Just as I did for orange, I am going to discuss green team actions in the context of the seven phases of the SDLC. As is the case with orange, the NICE Framework does not list any work roles that align to green teamers. Once again, I'm going to talk about this color slice in terms of on-the-job activities that should be *added* to *existing* work roles. Those same yellow team product managers, cloud architects, test engineers, DevOps managers, database administrators, and other jobs that have existed for decades need to authoritatively walk that thin blue line to build defensive attitudes as part of their daily functions.

Green teamers take the defenses of blue and mix them with the production of yellow to create resilience in IT systems. Professionals in these roles take the strategic plans, policies, and compliance requirements and proactively apply cybersecurity defenses in each phase. The purpose here is to ensure a secure digital asset is delivered to the production environment by the builders.

Green team activities are easiest to implement after some offensive or negative consequences are imagined. Once again, I recommend threat modeling as a sort of superpower to be harnessed here. The work roles in the green slice are the same as those in the orange slice since both are derivative of yellow team activities. It is my hope that orange and green jobs become more the norm, much like the purple team has in the past few years.

For the purposes of simplicity, I'll continue with the analogies previously used and focus the next section on the techniques and tactics to utilize for green teaming. Green teaming is all about putting defenses in place to prevent or mitigate problems in a proactive manner.

Plan/Define

Here product managers (and similar job functions) detail their use cases and sequence diagrams with specific defensive requirements. They can do this because they are aware of the risks of not doing so, and they have learned about the particular tools and techniques that are appropriate for the IT system they are defining. For example, if the system they're building will process credit card transactions, Payment Card Industry Data Security Standards (PCI-DSS) will apply; therefore, these three defensive requirements regarding crypto would likely be defined as part of the system build plan:

- Protect card data at rest—that is, in databases and data stores— with Advanced Encryption Standard (AES) encryption. AES is the recommended encryption method for PCI-DSS, HIPAA, GLBA, and other privacy regulations. Minimum encryption strength and methods approved and certified by the National Institute of Standards and Technology (NIST) provide assurance that your data is secured to the highest standards.

Secondary Colors: Interdisciplinary Cybersecurity Work Roles

- Protect data in motion—data during transmission—with Pretty Good Privacy (PGP) encryption. PGP is the standard for encrypted file exchange among the world's largest retail, finance, medical, industrial, and IT services companies.

- Protect encryption keys by keeping them apart from data stores. Leaving encrypted data and the keys used to en/decrypt it in the same location is akin to leaving the key to your house under a welcome mat by the front door. Security best practices require that you store encryption keys separately from encrypted data.

Design/Code

In orange teaming, I discussed a denial-of-service (DoS) attack on the e-commerce system you're designing. There, I mentioned that once an architect understands the potential of DoS attacks, they might opt to use a CSP's authentication service that allows for login monitoring and throttling of login attempts to thwart DoS attempts. Let's consider another example. Let's say the architect received red team training on the threat of cross-site scripting (XSS), and they understand the risk of reflective XSS in web applications (displaying user-provided input on a confirmation screen, for example, without first sanitizing it). A green teamer in this phase may decide to mandate two different defensive measures because they learned that XSS can be very damaging, and they now know the security principle of defense in depth. *Defense in depth* is nothing more than layering multiple security controls on top of one another in case one of them fails or is compromised by a malicious actor. This is a common activity in our daily lives. We lock the front door to our houses when we leave, but we also may set an alarm that would play a loud sound and notify police if someone were to break down the front door.

In the case of an e-commerce system, an IT architect may include a content security policy. A content security policy lets you define rules to protect users and apps from web attacks by providing a standard way of declaring approved origins of content that browsers are allowed to load.

Figure 4.2 shows how a content security policy works. The default domain is set to `example.com`, so if the user agent (browser) requests `index.js` or `index.css` from that domain, the resources are allowed to execute. However, when the browser tries to load `xyz.js` from a different domain, it is blocked. The content security policy restricts assets from loading from an unknown domain (which may be malicious).

Figure 4.2   How a content security policy works

As a secondary measure, the architect may explicitly include the `AntiXSS` library from .NET in application blueprints and sequence diagrams to ensure that all transactions that accept user input run through that particular sanitization routine before being sent to the backend servers. The `AntiXssEncoder` class encodes a string for use in HTML, XML, CSS, and URL processing. It's almost like having a guard booth on your driveway that makes sure people are filtered before they are allowed to pass through.

Build/Develop

For all encryption and XSS protections defined during the planning and design stages, almost nothing is more powerful than writing secure software code, if for no other reason than that software dominates almost every aspect of today's digital world. It is a truly omnipresent and seemingly omnipotent force. Though it may sound simple, building secure code (and its relative assembling secure systems) is quite a daunting task. It requires a significant investment in education coupled with a commitment to keep that content up-to-date with the latest attack trends, defensive coding techniques, and technology developments.

This green team activity is almost impossible to execute well unless you also have its orange team complement present. For many IT Sys-Dev teams, this is a major pitfall. Even when the "what" and "why" are well defined—one element taken from the example would be to encrypt data at rest because of the need to comply with PCI security standards—the "how" is often missing. Builders often don't know how to implement defenses into the systems they're constructing. This frequently takes the form of secure code training. However, given that today most business applications are more assembled than coded from scratch, it is equally important to procure or develop training related to the secure use of open-source software, third-party components, and commercial off-the-shelf software, as well as cloud services and APIs.

Continuing with the crypto example, a defensive builder/developer would take the time to create a data flow diagram (or refer to one if built by other team members) and review where data needs to be encrypted, decrypted, salted, hashed, and so on. Then they would use industry-standard crypto algorithms to secure that data at rest and in transit, taking care to use and store crypto keys from/in safe locations that can be separated by default from the data itself. This defensive coding is green teaming in action during the development phase.

Test/Validate

When it comes to the quality assurance testing phase, verification is the name of the game for green teamers. In this phase, the primary goal is to confirm and document that the defined, designed, and implemented security controls have been correctly executed. This green slice, ironically, harkens back to the days of quality assurance testers serving to verify IT system specifications. This group's success is largely driven by the groups that precede it in the seven phases. Of course, security controls won't always be planned, blueprinted, and built perfectly (and often not at all), so what is a green tester to do in the absence of good security requirements? Fortunately, there are a number of good resources to use as references. I'm going to list only one: OWASP's Application Security Verification Standard (ASVS).

ASVS provides a basis for testing technical security controls in IT systems and includes a list of requirements for secure development that can be shared with implementation teams. Though it was built initially and primarily intended for web applications, many of the concepts are applicable to nearly any platform, especially the security principles and foundational verification techniques. Fortunately, ASVS has content that discusses the role of automated security testing tools, manual penetration testing methods, and unit and integration tests. It is of highly leverageable utility to green teams for validation of authentication, access controls, data sanitization, cryptography, error handling, logging, and business logic. For those testers working on web, cloud, mobile, and IoT systems, it also has guidance on validating the security and integrity of APIs, web services, cloud configuration, and other dependencies.

To continue with the example, properly implemented input validation (for example, via the use of positive "allow lists" and strong data types) can eliminate more than 90 percent of injection attacks, including the XSS you're concerned about with your e-commerce system. Length and range checks done by green team testers can further reduce this threat. Related to this, output encoding is also critical to the security of any application; failing to encode output can result in an XSS-injectable application. Verifying output encoding is a perfect green test case, as you are positively validating the correct implementation of a security control built into the business application.

Release/Package

Similar to green team test and QA teams, release engineers who conduct green activities are all about verification and validation. The undertakings here are typically things like application integrity tests. As these work roles may have learned during their security awareness training, malicious code can still be inserted into an IT system during and after it is packaged and deployed. These applications need to protect themselves against attacks such as executing unsigned code from untrusted sources, subdomain takeovers, and poisoned update sources. This green team job is the bridge between development and operations in many organizations, and its task should be coincident with any new release, application build, or configuration change. The proactive defenses applied in these work functions include verifying the presence of auto-update features and obtaining those updated over secure channels that have been signed with approved cryptography. IT systems should also block attempts to execute code from modules, plugins, header include statements, or other libraries the originate from untrusted sources.

Deploy/Adopt

IT system deployment deals with the installation, configuration, and operation of business applications; and, just like the other six roles in the SDLC, there are steps to be taken here to ensure security. Green team members in this phase can vary broadly in their job responsibilities. They can range from being primarily responsible for identity and access management (IAM) controls (especially in cloud deployments) to simply validating that those controls work in the full production environment.

Let's assume the latter in this example and build on the access control analogy of the fictional home and e-commerce system. This role would be responsible for making sure the guard booth, front door, and alarm system are properly configured, staffed, and operational. The e-commerce system might need to use CSP IAM services to define hierarchies and segmentation for multiple levels of users and resources. With large organizations or environments that change frequently, this can be cumbersome. If your e-commerce system is deployed in Google Cloud, deployment green teamers are likely going to use GCP's Resource Manager (GCP RPM) to create and edit conditions for each group and what they can do on the system. For example, they may choose to allow or deny access based on variables such as time of day, type of resource attempting the access, resource name, and so on. They'll need to learn how to structure access controls and permissions in defensive ways; for example, *resource tags* in GCP RM are a way to simplify access control. A tag is a key-value pair that you attach to an organization, folder, or project. Figure 4.3 shows a simple example of how this works in Google Cloud. In the example, only members of the DevOps group can see assets in the Intranet and Web Apps folders; members of the Accounting group cannot.

These tags are attributes you assign to roles, jobs, departments, locations, types of workload, special cross-teams, or whatever other attributes make sense for your organization. Resource tags are helpful to manage granular permissions and are a good strategy for enforcing the principle of least privilege. Once you set a tag on a resource, you can create a conditional policy to allow or deny access based on that tag. Resources always inherit tags from parent resources, so, like permissions, they require careful planning—you can lock out a valid user seeking to perform legitimate actions if you're overzealous with your deployment controls.

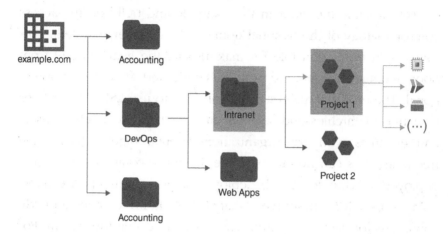

Figure 4.3 Using resource tags in Google Cloud for access control

Monitor/Observe

Green team monitors focus on the data that enables rapid response, feedback, metrics, and observability. They need to understand what anomalous behavior to look for and then "program" their deployment environment to track, log, and report on anything that falls outside of the normal range (however that is defined). To complete the house and e-commerce application examples, green teamers in this phase are analogous to motion cameras that activate and log something we don't expect to "see." For cloud-deployed IT systems, we'll use GCP again, although all CSPs have similar functionality. Google Cloud Logging works across all Google Cloud services and integrates with monitoring, error reporting, and cloud trace services. You can use Cloud Logging to securely store, analyze, report on, and create alerts for logged events. Log dashboards allow you to view charts, aggregate metrics, and even stream logs that meet the criteria you specify. Setting up a "trip wire" to log and proactively report on any overload of login attempts to your e-commerce system is a perfect example to close the loop, so to speak. These will be the most useful for ensuring the integrity of your DevOps activities.

Actions and activities labeled as "green teaming" encompass aspects of defensive collaboration, coordination, and a holistic approach to building security into the system development life cycle. This emerging field is still relegated to the realm of training yellow team members on defensive security tactics, but as the cybersecurity color wheel continues to evolve, a spectrum of responsibilities will merge to create cohesive work roles that manifest as green. Much like purple teaming has become a movement in cybersecurity, I believe those individuals and organizations that proactively take a green team approach will be advantaged in their careers and companies. They will also better equip their respective enterprises to fight cybercrime more effectively.

Security Champions

In the secondary color world, and in particular, for the orange and green activities that are adjacent to yellow, the concept of *security champions* is a powerful tool to have in your war chest. Security champions are yellow team members who have or develop specialized security skills. They are valuable because they are already yellow team members; hence, there is immediate credibility and trust conveyed to their peers. They can educate IT staff on how to plan for security requirements and reinforce the importance of integrating security into each of the seven phases of development and delivery.

Security champions fast-track an organization's ability to adopt security activities in non-security-first groups like yellow teams because they enable the organization to identify potential design or implementation problems in IT system development processes. They can also work with implementation, release, deployment, and

Secondary Colors: Interdisciplinary Cybersecurity Work Roles

monitoring teams to provide remediation, defense in depth, and rapid response. The exact duties and responsibilities of security champions vary from organization to organization; but, they should reflect the priorities and team style into which they're embedded.

If you want to be a security champion or build a security champion program at your organization, a commitment to initial training and ongoing development is necessary. To establish proficiency and uniformity through skills training and ensure both competency and consistency among security champions, it is imperative to provide them with comprehensive security skills training that includes formal education and hands-on practice. Rather than solely relying on elements like computer-based training, leaders should strive to foster dynamic discussions that revolve around real-world challenges routinely encountered by their development teams. Furthermore, IT leaders can institute a recognition program that celebrates significant training milestones and skill development achievements. For instance, they may assign distinct "belts" to each security champion to symbolize their level of expertise and acknowledge their continuous progress, as depicted in Table 4.1 (geared for orange team Security Champions).

Table 4.1 Creating Security Champions with Belt Programs

Belt or Tier	Basic Training	Advanced Training	On-the-Job Actions
Yellow	OWASP top 10 web threats	Play a basic capture-the-flag (CTF) game on a cyber range.	Five code sprints with no high-priority security vulnerabilities.

Belt or Tier	Basic Training	Advanced Training	On-the-Job Actions
Brown	Language and platform-specific attacks	Complete five CTFs and place in top 10 at least once.	Train other yellow teamers on security basics.
Black	Industry certification in offensive skills, e.g., OSCP	Closed loop training for top five security threats to your IT system: ID flaw via attack, fix flaw, demonstrate attack no longer successful in production environment.	Author secure coding guidelines.

It is paramount that the security champion training program aligns closely with the specific demands of the security team (red and blue teamers), as well as the platforms, tools, and applications in use. Collaborative efforts among security teams, infrastructure and operations personnel, and application leaders are indispensable for ensuring the ongoing advancement of security champions and the continued relevance of training to meet the evolving demands of the business.

Summary

The analogy between colors and roles detailed in these previous two chapters serves as a reminder that cybersecurity is not a solitary endeavor; rather, it is a collective effort that requires the expertise and cooperation of various professionals across many job functions. As the digital landscape continues to evolve, this unique perspective underscores the intricate dance of colors and roles that shape the ever-changing cybersecurity canvas.

Ideally, this analogy has simplified and clarified the complex world of cybersecurity for you a little bit. I cannot overstress the importance of collaboration, innovation, strategic planning, and creative thinking in safeguarding your digital assets, people, and world. The lens of the cybersecurity color wheel is a framework that I trust will inspire you to cooperate, modernize, organize, and think creatively when it comes to integrating cybersecurity into your plans.

For cybersecurity professionals, the potential of purple teaming is massive—both as a stand-alone profession and a collaborative effort between red and blue teams. Red and blue teamers also have the opportunity (some would say obligation) to expose their yellow team colleagues to the ways of offensive and defensive security as a means to harden the IT systems constructed and operated by those yellow teams.

Leaders in HR, IT, and cybersecurity should recognize the incredible value that can be added to their respective teams by practicing some proactive color blending and engaging in cross-team training endeavors. You may discover hidden talent among your staff and identify security gaps you never knew existed in your teams or infrastructure.

Chapter 5

The Guiding Light: "White" Cybersecurity Work Roles from the Color Wheel

For all the building, breaking, and defending going on in any given enterprise, there needs to be some form of guiderails. These recipes are provided by a group I refer to as the "bakers." These are the people who collect, collate, and disseminate the security and privacy requirements placed on the enterprise. These requirements can be derived from customers, regulators, laws, compliance mandates, and other forms of governance. This is a critically important and often overlooked role for cybersecurity. Job seekers who want to be in cyber but don't want a heavy technical role should look to be a baker. There is a heavy focus on risk assessment, compliance management, and security oversight.

Privacy has emerged as a strong force in this group as well, fueled by the omnipresence of laws like the *General Data Protection Regulation* (GDPR) and the *California Consumer Privacy Act* (*CCPA*). Privacy implications for builders and defenders are highly relevant and far too often ignored or misunderstood. Bakers are associated with the color of a kitchen apron—white. They sit at the center of my color wheel because they touch every other color in some manner.

Sniffing Out the Bakers

In Chapter 2, I listed 50 cybersecurity jobs that are either common or trending in the industry. Of those jobs, these are the ones I consider to be part of the "bakers" (aka makers)—the policy creators, governors, watchers, and guides who set the stage for the work done by the various color slices:

- **Artificial intelligence security specialist:** Uses AI to combat cybercrime
- **Cybersecurity Scrum master:** Watches over and protects all data
- **Chief information security officer (CISO):** Head honcho of cybersecurity
- **Chief security officer (CSO):** Heads up all physical/info/cybersecurity
- **Cyber insurance policy specialist:** Consults on cyber risk and liability protection
- **Cybersecurity lawyer:** Attorney focused on info/cybersecurity and cybercrime
- **Data privacy officer:** Ensures legal compliance related to data protection
- **Data recovery specialist:** Recovers hacked data from digital devices
- **Governance, compliance, and risk (GRC) manager:** Oversees risk management
- **Security auditor:** Conducts audits on an organization's information systems

In its *Security Trends 2023* report, Techstrong Research wrote this:

"The backlash against shift left forces security to question whether it's too onerous to expect developers to take responsibility for building security into the application.

It's time we rethink the shift left philosophy and find something that works for everyone."

While I agree with this assessment, the question is which work roles are tasked with doing that rethinking and finding a solution that works for everyone? The white apron-clad bakers, of course!

These leaders are chartered, not with protecting the digital assets of their organizations, per se; rather, they are commissioned with aligning cybersecurity strategy with business risk. The NICE Framework lacks white team work roles defined as such; however, let me call attention to several actual job titles taken from organizations including Fidelity Investments, Biogen, Capital One, Cedars-Sinai, UCLA, TikTok, and NTT Global:

- Director of technology risk
- Digital risk control expert
- Cloud security GRC specialist
- IT governance analyst
- IT risk compliance manager
- GRC analyst
- Compliance and audit analyst

Many of these jobs call for familiarity with specific security frameworks, such as ISO/IEC 2700x, PCI-DSS, CobiT, ITIL, NIST 800-53, GDPR, HIPAA, and others. Job seekers can add to their value by learning one or more of these frameworks. There are many training organizations that offer courses and exam preparation for valuable industry certifications—e.g., Certified Information Security System Professional (CISSP)—that also require knowledge of these same security frameworks.

The practitioner-level jobs listed here require only fundamental knowledge of cybersecurity principles such as access control, cryptography, physical and environmental security, systems acquisition and development, security incident management, and business continuity. Most of these jobs are not particularly technical in nature. In fact, backgrounds in finance, philosophy, and communications are often quite useful in these roles because you'll be asked to assess the value of investments, determine the trade-offs, and consider compensating controls with respect to risk.

Organizations that hire and develop these work roles vary wildly in where the jobs sit organizationally. Some are in information security teams, others in technology or IT teams, and others still in legal. This is an area where both we as an industry and the NICE Framework itself need further development and alignment.

The practitioner-level jobs listed in this chapter often go unfilled (and sometimes not even applied for) because the hiring managers and HR professionals involved in the creation of the job description's roles and responsibilities are influenced by IT, security, and other teams to include technology requirements that are mostly not necessary. This disqualifies and discourages perfectly competent individuals from applying, further exacerbating the very problem they're trying to resolve.

CISO as Proxy for Cyber Staff

Since many people in cybersecurity aspire to be a CISO, let me take the time to discuss 10 critically important white team job functions a CISO has. For those leaders and executives planning to recruit, retain, and develop cybersecurity talent, consider integrating some of these functions into existing jobs or breaking apart the CISO's job into multiple deputized roles that can round out your cyber resilience and bolster your team's capabilities.

CISOs obviously play a crucial role in an organization's cybersecurity hygiene that goes well beyond offensive and defensive activities. Here are my choices for top roles and responsibilities of a CISO that are not directly related to red team or blue team activities:

- **Developing cybersecurity policies and procedures:** CISOs are responsible for establishing and maintaining cybersecurity policies, standards, and procedures that align with the organization's goals and regulatory requirements.

- **Cybersecurity governance:** CISOs ensure that the organization's cybersecurity strategy is aligned with its overall business goals and objectives. This includes providing cybersecurity guidance to executive leadership and the board of directors.

- **Risk management:** CISOs are tasked with identifying, assessing, and mitigating cybersecurity risks. They develop risk management strategies to protect the organization's digital assets and data.

- **Compliance and regulatory compliance:** Ensuring that the organization complies with relevant cybersecurity regulations and standards is a significant responsibility. CISOs must stay up-to-date with evolving compliance requirements.

- **Security awareness and training:** Promoting a culture of cybersecurity awareness among employees is crucial. CISOs oversee security training programs and awareness campaigns to educate all employees about potential threats and best practices.

- **Vendor and third-party risk programs:** Many organizations rely on third-party vendors for various services. CISOs are responsible for assessing and managing the cybersecurity risks associated with these external partnerships.

- **Incident response planning:** Developing and maintaining an effective incident response plan is vital. CISOs ensure that the organization is well-prepared to respond to cybersecurity incidents, minimizing their impact.

- **Security auditing and assessment:** Regularly auditing and assessing the organization's security posture helps identify vulnerabilities and weaknesses. CISOs coordinate these assessments and ensure that necessary improvements are made.

- **Security budget management:** Managing the cybersecurity budget is a key responsibility. CISOs allocate resources effectively to address security needs, procure tools and technologies, and invest in talent development.

- **Security reporting and communication:** CISOs communicate cybersecurity information to various stakeholders, including executive leadership, employees, and external partners. They provide updates on the organization's security posture and incidents, emphasizing the importance of cybersecurity.

These roles and responsibilities are critical for a CISO to effectively protect an organization's digital assets, reputation, and overall security posture. They also need appropriate staff and budget with which to execute these responsibilities. While offensive and defensive activities are essential components of cybersecurity, the broader responsibilities of a CISO ensure a comprehensive and strategic approach to cybersecurity management. Red, blue, and other colors emerge from the policies, strategy, and vision created and maintained by the office of the CISO.

Cybersecurity Law, Insurance, and Audit

Job roles related to cybersecurity law, insurance, and audit also play pivotal roles in ensuring the security and compliance of organizations in our increasingly digital world. These roles are essential components of a comprehensive cybersecurity strategy, helping businesses mitigate risks, comply with regulations, adhere to regional laws, and recover from cyber incidents.

Cybersecurity Law

Cybersecurity lawyers, also known as cyber attorneys or information security lawyers, specialize in the legal aspects of cybersecurity. They play a critical role in advising organizations on cyber-related legal issues. The responsibilities of cybersecurity lawyers encompass regulatory compliance, where they assist businesses in navigating intricate cybersecurity regulations and standards to ensure legal adherence, as well as data breach response, involving the development and execution of response plans in case of data breaches, including guiding organizations through notification and disclosure procedures. They also handle contract review by evaluating and drafting cybersecurity-related contracts, such as vendor agreements, to safeguard the organization's interests. Additionally, cybersecurity lawyers may provide litigation support, representing the organization in legal proceedings or disputes arising from cyberattacks or breaches.

Cybersecurity Insurance

Cybersecurity insurance professionals work in the insurance industry to assess, underwrite, and manage cybersecurity risks for policyholders. In the realm of cybersecurity insurance, professionals fulfill a multifaceted role that includes risk assessment, involving the evaluation of an organization's cybersecurity stance to determine suitable coverage and premiums. They engage in policy development by collaborating with underwriters to craft cybersecurity insurance policies tailored to individual client requirements. These experts also manage claims, efficiently processing them in the event of a cybersecurity incident, while closely collaborating with policyholders and incident response teams. Furthermore, they play a pivotal role in educating clients about the advantages of cybersecurity insurance and facilitating comprehension of policy terms and conditions.

Cybersecurity Audit

Cybersecurity auditors, often known as information security auditors or compliance auditors, focus on evaluating and assessing an organization's security controls and practices. Within the domain of cybersecurity audit, professionals assume a multifaceted role involving assessment and testing and encompassing the execution of audits and security assessments to pinpoint vulnerabilities and weaknesses within an organization's cybersecurity infrastructure. They also oversee compliance verification, assuring that the organization aligns with pertinent cybersecurity regulations, standards, and internal policies. Furthermore, they offer valuable recommendations and solutions for enhancing security posture while ensuring the resolution of identified issues. Their duties extend to producing comprehensive audit reports that encapsulate findings, risks, and recommended actions for the benefit of stakeholders.

In summary, these job roles in cybersecurity law, insurance, and audit contribute significantly to safeguarding organizations from cyber threats, ensuring legal compliance, and managing risk. They are essential components of a holistic cybersecurity strategy, helping businesses navigate the complex landscape of cybersecurity threats and regulations while minimizing financial and legal liabilities.

An Oldie and a Newie, but Both Goodies

A *cybersecurity Scrum master* is a specialized role within the field of cybersecurity that combines the principles of *Scrum*, an agile project management framework, with the specific needs and challenges of managing cybersecurity initiatives. It's a very cool job that combines proven, effective, cutting-edge project management that has its origins in software development to the world of (mostly) defensive cybersecurity. It's a greenish kind of role, but pale enough that I include it here. Cybersecurity Scrum masters serve as facilitators for agile practices in the cybersecurity team. They help the team understand and implement agile methodologies and Scrum principles to improve their efficiency and effectiveness. This is particularly useful for backlog management and the prioritization of security-related tasks based on risk and business needs. Collaboration and communication with other stakeholders are also a key responsibility to help ensure that all team members are aligned on cybersecurity goals and tasks. This involves continuous cyber improvement, serving as security champion for nonsecurity teams, and owning the reporting and metrics function for overall cybersecurity program tracking. They often work with the CISO's team to establish and track key performance indicators (KPIs) and metrics related to cybersecurity efforts, providing regular updates to management and stakeholders.

As you can see, the world of cybersecurity is rich with opportunity. Some of these jobs have existed for a long time, some are newly emerging, and the exciting world of uncolored (white) cyber work has its own unique type of value to provide to the enterprise.

Summary

This chapter introduced the concept of white teams, which are cybersecurity work roles from the color wheel that I refer to as "the guiding light." It offers an insightful exploration into the often overlooked but crucial aspect of cybersecurity—the role of "bakers." These professionals are responsible for setting cybersecurity and privacy requirements for enterprises, derived from various sources such as customers, regulators, and laws. This role, symbolized by the color white and likened to a kitchen apron, is essential yet frequently underestimated in the cybersecurity realm.

Bakers focus on business risk assessment, compliance management, and security oversight, making this role suitable to those interested in cybersecurity without a heavy technical focus. There is a growing importance of privacy within this group, especially with regulations like GDPR and CCPA. These bakers interact with every other aspect of cybersecurity, making their role central and interconnected.

Several cybersecurity jobs are categorized under bakers, including AI security specialists, cybersecurity Scrum masters, CISOs, CSOs, cyber insurance policy specialists, cybersecurity lawyers, and others. Each of these roles contributes uniquely to the overarching cybersecurity strategies of organizations.

Techstrong Research's Security Trends 2023 report highlights the need for rethinking the "shift left" philosophy in cybersecurity, a task falling under the purview of bakers. These professionals are tasked with aligning cybersecurity strategy with business risk, rather than just protecting digital assets.

Job titles like director of technology risk, digital risk control expert, and others are mentioned, emphasizing the need for familiarity with various security frameworks. Job seekers can increase their value by learning these frameworks.

The chapter further discussed the often-neglected practitioner-level jobs in cybersecurity, which don't require heavy technical knowledge. Skills from finance, philosophy, and communications are useful in these roles.

The roles and responsibilities of a CISO are important beyond just offensive and defensive cybersecurity activities. These responsibilities include developing cybersecurity policies, governance, risk management, compliance, security awareness training, and more.

Finally, the chapter addressed the pivotal roles of cybersecurity law, insurance, and audit in an organization's cybersecurity strategy. These include cyber attorneys, cybersecurity insurance professionals, and cybersecurity auditors, each playing a critical role in legal compliance, risk management, and assessment of security controls.

Overall, this chapter attempted to shed light on the diverse range of roles within the cybersecurity sector, emphasizing the importance of the white roles in shaping and guiding cybersecurity strategies and policies. I advocate for a broader understanding of cybersecurity jobs, encouraging job seekers to explore these vital yet often underrepresented roles in the industry.

Cybersecurity Roles in Action

Part II of this book provides three specialty chapters intended to provide real-world context to working in the cybersecurity industry. The topics cover the prevailing technology that powers our digital world, the role of diversity in providing better security to our enterprises, and advice distilled from nearly 150 leaders and practitioners.

Chapter 6 is dedicated to software's omnipresence and importance in cybersecurity and our daily lives. It is difficult to exist in today's modern world without depending on software in some capacity. When it comes to cybersecurity and emerging technology trends, like artificial intelligence, software is the dominant player. Knowing how to interact with, integrate, develop, and use software securely is absolutely paramount to safe cyber operations.

Chapter 7 addresses a problem and an opportunity facing the cybersecurity industry: lack of diverse talent. There are many underrepresented demographics in cybersecurity. Homogenous organizations are plagued by a lack of innovation and uninspiring cyber solutions compared to more heterogeneous groups (including cyber criminals). The chapter provides a practical framework and actionable strategies companies can adopt to improve diversity and inclusion among their cybersecurity talent pools.

Chapter 8 is a broad-reaching discussion of case studies, advice, and survey analysis collected over nearly a year. It presents snippets from interviews, informal discussions, collaborations, and research data into pragmatic advice. You learn what hiring managers seek in entry-level candidates, read about challenges faced by practitioners and leaders in our field, and receive advice about how to begin a cybersecurity career. I conclude the chapter, and the book, with five case studies to highlight examples of the many ways to build value for yourself and your employer with respect to a cybersecurity career.

Chapter 6

Software: The Catalyst of Today's Digital Enterprise

In our modern era, the bedrock of our digital existence is none other than software. It's not just our phones or computers; it's our homes, our vehicles, and the entire infrastructure of commerce and the very essence of our communication networks. Software's omnipresence has ushered in an era of unparalleled convenience through the on-demand economy, but it has also expanded the attack surface for malicious actors.

As our world becomes increasingly interconnected and perpetually online, the scope of what's at risk has transcended mere digital data. We now face a reality where much more hangs in the balance, demanding an elevated commitment to safeguarding and fortifying our digital infrastructure.

The traditional demarcation lines between the cyber and physical realms are rapidly blurring. If we adhere to the axiom that safety hinges on security, the urgency of bolstering software security becomes glaringly apparent.

Software's Ubiquitous Relevance to Cybersecurity

The significance of software to cybersecurity cannot be overstated. With the exponential growth of interconnected devices, networks, and systems, the potential vulnerabilities and threats have similarly escalated. At the heart of this cybersecurity paradigm lies software, playing a pivotal role in both transforming our lives but also safe-guarding sensitive information, critical infrastructure, and personal data. The relevance of software in cybersecurity is not limited to just one facet; rather, it spans a multitude of dimensions including prevention, detection, response, and recovery. Software drives our global digital world, and thus it needs to be secured. This chapter explores the importance of software security and discusses how we can harden it during construction and leverage it to shape the future of digital protection.

Cyber threats have become increasingly sophisticated, ranging from traditional malware to advanced persistent threats (APTs) and zero-day exploits. In response, cybersecurity professionals have turned to software as a primary line of defense. Antivirus and anti-malware software, for instance, constantly update their threat data-bases to identify and neutralize the latest malware strains. Intrusion detection and prevention systems utilize software algorithms to mon-itor network traffic, flagging suspicious patterns and behaviors that may indicate a breach attempt. The dynamic nature of cyber threats demands agile and adaptive software solutions that can stay ahead of potential attackers.

APTs and Zero-Day Exploits

Advanced persistent threats are a type of cyberattack character-ized by their sophisticated level, prolonged duration, and tar-geted focus. These attacks are typically conducted by highly skilled and well-resourced threat actors, such as nation-states or state-sponsored groups, aiming to steal, modify, or disrupt data and information systems.

Zero-day exploits are cyberattacks that take advantage of a pre-viously unknown vulnerability in software or hardware. The term

---

zero-day denotes that the developers of the vulnerable system have had zero days to address and patch the vulnerability since it was first discovered and exploited by attackers. These vulnerabilities are highly valuable to attackers because there is no available patch or direct defense against them at the time of the exploit.

Secure communication forms the channel of many digital interactions, ranging from email exchanges to financial transactions. Encryption software, using complex algorithms, ensures that sensitive information is transformed into unreadable code during transmission, only to be deciphered by authorized recipients. Virtual private networks (VPNs) employ software to create encrypted tunnels, safeguarding the confidentiality of data exchanged between remote locations. Additionally, secure messaging applications rely on end-to-end encryption to prevent unauthorized access to messages, ensuring the privacy of individuals and organizations alike. This all requires specialized knowledge and training for those who build, operate, update, and defend these communication networks between interconnected systems and devices.

Identity and access management (IAM) plays a crucial role in cybersecurity by regulating who can access what information within a network or system. IAM is paramount to defining and controlling the simple, yet difficult to secure, concepts of who a user is (identify) and what that user can do (access). Software-based IAM solutions enforce strong authentication protocols, including multifactor authentication (MFA), biometrics, and smart cards, to ensure that only authorized users can gain entry. Role-based access control (RBAC) is another software-driven concept that assigns permissions based on job roles, limiting access to sensitive data to only those who require it. By integrating IAM software, organizations can mitigate the risks associated with unauthorized access and identity theft.

Software-Defined Security

Software-defined security has emerged as a transformative concept, enabling the dynamic adaptation of security measures to match the evolving threat landscape. Through software-defined networks and software-defined perimeters, organizations can segment their networks, ensuring that each segment has its security protocols tailored to its specific needs. This approach enhances resilience against lateral movement by attackers and minimizes the potential impact of breaches. It also isolates more critical systems, allowing teams to deploy more stringent controls based on risk ratings. By utilizing software to define security parameters, organizations can swiftly adjust their defenses in response to emerging threats, enhancing overall cyber resilience.

Earlier in the book, I discussed the concept of threat hunting, a proactive cybersecurity approach that involves actively searching for signs of malicious activities in an organization's network. Software-driven threat hunting tools leverage advanced analytics and behavior-based algorithms to detect subtle signs of compromise, allowing cybersecurity professionals to identify and neutralize threats before they escalate. Of course, operators need to be able to tweak these software tools to fine-tune their threat intelligence gathering, which means knowledge of software (not necessarily coding but perhaps scripting and/or software-based configuration) becomes a required enabler to threat hunting. These software-driven approaches enable the continuous monitoring of systems, networks, and endpoints, ensuring that potential vulnerabilities are addressed promptly and breaches are mitigated effectively.

Training for Software Security

The human element, of course, remains a critical factor in cybersecurity, with human error often contributing to successful cyberattacks.

Software plays a significant role in training and awareness programs, educating employees and users about the best practices for maintaining digital hygiene. Interactive e-learning modules, phishing simulation software, and security awareness platforms are all examples of software-based solutions that educate individuals about the risks associated with cyber threats. It's the easiest way to scale a security awareness training program. By utilizing software-driven training tools, organizations can empower their workforce to become the first line of defense against cyber threats. When considering security awareness, you need to be mindful to include the builders, those who define and construct the IT systems and applications the enterprise depends on. Builders need specialized training specific to their work role and technology stack. For example, a front-end Java developer needs very different training than a quality assurance engineer. The importance of role-based training for technical development teams cannot be overstated.

Software-Driven Security

Despite best efforts, no organization can be completely immune to cyber incidents. In such scenarios, software-driven incident response and recovery processes become indispensable. Incident response platforms assist in assessing the extent of a breach, isolating affected systems, and coordinating remediation efforts. Backup and recovery software ensures that critical data can be restored in the aftermath of a breach, minimizing downtime and potential data loss. The efficiency of incident response and recovery relies heavily on software solutions that streamline the process and enable organizations to bounce back swiftly.

In the digital age, where the threat landscape is dynamic and ever-evolving, the role of software in cybersecurity is paramount. From protecting against an array of cyber threats to securing communication channels and enhancing identity management, software is at the forefront of cybersecurity efforts. Automation, artificial intelligence, and threat hunting tools further elevate the efficacy of cybersecurity strategies, while training and awareness software empower individuals to be more cyber-resilient. As the digital landscape continues to evolve, the relevance of software in all aspects of cybersecurity will only increase, driving innovation and shaping the future of secure digital interactions.

Software Is Unavoidable

For job seekers, I'm not saying you need to be a software developer to have a career in cybersecurity; far from it. I am saying that you need to have a fundamental understanding of how software functions and fails. This will equip you with the basic, yet necessary, skills to evaluate software risks in your organization.

For hiring managers and executives, the presence of software in almost every significant IT system is ineluctable. Incorporate software skills in as many job descriptions as reasonably make sense. Cross-reference the NICE work role KSAs and tasks for jobs that closely align to the positions you seek to hire. Discuss with peers in that group the role of software in their daily work lives. Software's impact is growing by the day; it is time to get caught up or risk falling even further behind.

The Role of Artificial Intelligence in Cybersecurity

The advent of automation and artificial intelligence (AI) can potentially revolutionize cybersecurity, empowering defenders to analyze vast amounts of data and identify patterns that humans might miss. Machine learning algorithms, a subset of AI, can detect anomalies in network behavior, indicating potential breaches or unauthorized activities. Similarly, automated incident response systems can use predefined software-based playbooks to take immediate actions in the event of a security incident, minimizing response times and reducing human error. The relevance of software-driven automation and AI is evident in its ability to scale defenses, even in the face of an increasingly complex threat landscape. Let me be clear—this day is not here quite yet. Current incantations of AI are fun and useful for helping humans improve code, analyze healthcare imaging, guide cars while driving, crunch big data sets, and provide predictive customer service on websites. But one thing is perfectly clear and current ...

Artificial intelligence *is* software. This means it is flexible, scalable, and can be powered by the cloud; but, it is also fallible, prone to make errors, and inherently insecure because it is created by humans. AI can be weaponized for evil as easily as it can be supercharged for good using the power of software development and the scale of the cloud. But AI also has another risk—self modification. This is a real threat to self-improving AI. In fact, there have been instances where two AI systems communicating with each other created their own language because it was more efficient to share information and improvement ideas that way. This new language was indecipherable to the humans who created the AI systems, and they ultimately had to shut it down for fear of not knowing how the AI might transform.

Whereas the proliferation of data and the increasing sophistication of cyber threats have propelled cybersecurity to the forefront of organizational priorities, the same is true for AI. As traditional security measures struggle to keep pace, a new weapon has emerged for the defenders: artificial intelligence. By harnessing the power of AI, cybersecurity professionals are gaining a powerful ally in their battle against cyber adversaries. But as illustrated, AI is multifaceted and can pose threats to organizations as well as benefits to cybersecurity professionals.

121

Top AI Threats to Organizations

Cybercriminals have become more sophisticated, using advanced tactics to bypass traditional security measures. Consider some of the top threats that companies face:

- **Advanced persistent threats:** APTs are stealthy, prolonged attacks that target specific organizations or individuals. Attackers use custom malware and methods to infiltrate networks, steal sensitive data, and maintain access for extended periods. The SolarWinds hack, wherein attackers compromised the software build process to embed malicious code, is a poignant example of how APTs can be both broad-reaching and elusive if the payload is hidden cleverly, as it was in the SolarWinds attack. APTs can be weaponized with AI. Once an APT gains access to a target network, it can wait for just the right opportunity before launching its payload while learning common network behaviors so it can better emulate a legitimate user to avoid intrusion detection systems.

- **Zero-day exploits:** Better known as *zero days*, these are weaknesses in software that are exploited by attackers before developers can release a patch. These have been around since the dawn of IT, and they can cause significant damage, as there are no immediate solutions to mitigate the risks. AI-powered advanced scanning and reconnaissance technologies have made finding zero days much easier.

- **Phishing attacks:** Phishing remains a popular attack vector, using social engineering to trick individuals into revealing sensitive information or installing malware. As phishing attacks become more convincing, employees are increasingly at risk of falling victim. AI is particularly useful here to make the attack vectors—a fake email or text message—seem much more authentic.

- **Ransomware attacks:** Ransomware attacks encrypt an organization's data and demand a ransom in exchange for the decryption key. These attacks can lead to data loss, operational disruption, and financial losses. Sadly, ransomware has been proven to cause human loss of life in situations where a hospital's IT system was shut down and ambulances with patients in critical conditions en route had to be rerouted to other healthcare facilities; these patients perished before they could reach the next hospital. AI can be used in conjunction with ransomware to better estimate the limits of what a target is willing to pay, increasing the likelihood of a payout for the attacker.

Potential Security Benefits of AI

The integration of AI technologies can also provide significant benefits toward revolutionizing the field of cybersecurity. It offers numerous advantages that empower cybersecurity professionals to stay ahead of the aforementioned evolving threats.

- **Real-time threat detection:** AI-powered tools can analyze vast amounts of data in real time, enabling the rapid detection of anomalies and suspicious activities. By identifying deviations from normal behavior, AI algorithms can alert security teams to potential threats, allowing for prompt intervention. Of course, considering that AI can also be used to avoid such detection, we're on the precipice of another cyber arms race.

- **Enhanced malware detection:** AI-driven malware detection tools can identify malicious patterns and behaviors that traditional antivirus software might miss. Machine learning models can evolve as they encounter new threats, improving accuracy over time.

- **Behavioral analysis:** AI enables behavioral analysis, which involves monitoring user and network activities for deviations from established norms. This heuristic approach can uncover insider threats and APTs that evade traditional signature-based methods.

- **Automated incident responses:** AI can automate incident response workflows, enabling rapid containment and mitigation of threats. Automated responses can isolate compromised systems, minimize damage, and reduce the time it takes to neutralize threats.

- **Predictive analytics:** AI can provide predictive analytics to anticipate potential security threats by analyzing historical data and identifying patterns. This proactive approach allows organizations to mitigate risks before they escalate.

- **Adaptive authentication:** Authentication systems can be supercharged to learn users' behavioral patterns and enhance accurate identity verification. This reduces the risk of unauthorized access, especially when combined with multifactor authentication.

Of course, all of these benefits and augmentations need to be programmed. That means software engineers and data scientists will play an increasingly important role in cybersecurity, specifically in the dominion of artificial intelligence and machine learning.

Other AI-Specific Concerns

It's crucial to acknowledge a few other potential challenges and drawbacks of AI through the lens of cybersecurity. Because AI is software itself, hackers can develop AI-driven attacks that exploit vulnerabilities in AI algorithms and models, enabling them to change outcomes presented by AI and/or bypass AI-built defenses.

The realm of privacy concerns is an interesting one with respect to AI, and I'm sure there are many privacy and legal professionals that will continue to debate this for years. AI is already monitoring a lot of what humans do, say, and read. Think of Apple's Siri, Amazon's Alexa, or other personal device and home IoT conveniences with AI built into it. Those systems listen to conversations, learn from behaviors, and proactively push sales offers that advertisers pay for, as a relatively harmless example. Imagine how else one's privacy might be compromised with similar systems. If those systems are used at work, in many instances the worker's privacy rights are virtually non-existent if the equipment used is owned by the employer and used on the employer's network. Striking the right balance between security and privacy is essential.

Finally, artificial intelligence comes with the risk of bias and discrimination. If not carefully designed, AI systems can inherit biases present in the data and humans used to train it, leading to unfair outcomes and discriminatory practices for which the owner of that AI may be liable.

As the AI landscape continues to evolve, so do the strategies employed by both cyber adversaries and cybersecurity practitioners. By harnessing the capabilities of AI, cybersecurity professionals can enhance threat detection, automate incident response, and bolster defenses against a variety of cyber threats. While the potential benefits of AI are immense, organizations must remain vigilant in addressing challenges and ethical concerns while recognizing that their adversaries are equally well-equipped with AI technology. By leveraging the power of AI responsibly, software and cybersecurity professionals can strengthen their defenses and ensure a safer digital future.

The Cloud Is Software Too!

Just as I argue that artificial intelligence is essentially software and that you cannot reap the benefits of AI without being knowledgeable about and dependent upon software engineering, I similarly claim that cloud security is also essentially equivalent to software security.

Cloud security software refers to the tools and technologies used to protect data, applications, and infrastructure in cloud computing environments. I consider it a subset of overall software security because it specifically focuses on securing cloud-based assets and mitigating the risks associated with cloud computing. However, keep in mind that the cloud services, APIs, and infrastructure (servers, networks, etc.) are all software—either in its entirety or mostly so.

Software security plays a crucial role in ensuring the overall security of cloud environments. Cloud computing relies on software systems to manage and secure data, applications, and infrastructure. The security of these software systems directly impacts the security of "the cloud" because it basically *is* the cloud.

Cloud Security Is Software Security

There are several reasons why I consider cloud security part of software security:

- **Encryption and data protection:** Software security provides encryption and data protection mechanisms to safeguard sensitive data in the cloud. Encryption ensures that data is securely transmitted and stored, reducing the risk of unauthorized interception or data breaches. The algorithms, key stores, and implementation protocols are all provided by the cloud service provider (CSP). Proper key management, secure protocols, and strong encryption algorithms are essential components of security in the cloud, and they are all either software you need to configure or integrate with via an application programming interface (API). This helps ensure the confidentiality, integrity, and availability of data stored in the cloud. Other access controls and data loss prevention (DLP) mechanisms that protect sensitive information from unauthorized access also require software programming or configuration. This means implementing encryption and DLP techniques to protect sensitive data within cloud environments—both encrypting data at rest and in transit, ensuring that even if data is intercepted or compromised, it remains unreadable without the proper decryption keys.

- **Application security:** Cloud-based applications are vulnerable to various security threats, such as cross-site scripting, injection attacks, and unauthorized access ... just as there are if sitting in a data center, on a private network, or on a server in your utility closet. Deploying an application to the cloud does not make it any more or less secure than it was prior. Applications don't live in isolation; they require data, networking services, security protections, and communication channels. Many of these services may now be provided by the CSP. Cloud security software provides tools for application-level networking, security, and data, such as web application firewalls, crypto systems, networking ports, and vulnerability scanning. All of these things need to be set up, organized, monitored, and tuned to protect cloud-hosted applications and ensure proper availability of services. These valuable CSP-provided tools are, again, almost always software.

- **Infrastructure as code (IaC):** This refers to the provisioning and management of your networking infrastructure via software code rather than a manual processes. Leveraging IaC, you make files that contain infrastructure specifications that can then be automatically built by the CSP. This is akin to the requirements and design specifications discussed earlier in this chapter when building software applications. This makes it easier to edit and distribute configurations. The CSPs safeguard the underlying infrastructure of cloud computing, which includes virtual machines, networks, storage, and other resources. It involves measures like network security controls, intrusion detection systems, and identity and access management (IAM) to secure the cloud infrastructure from attacks and unauthorized usage. But if you configure your IaC with a vulnerability, it will be propagated to every instance. And remember that all of those CSP safeguards still need to be set up and managed as software applications and/or APIs.

- **Software-powered GRC in the cloud:** CSPs help organizations adhere to regulatory requirements and industry standards related to data privacy and security because they offer software applications with features such as audit logs, security monitoring, and compliance reporting to ensure that cloud deployments meet the necessary legal and regulatory obligations. These applications need to be integrated into your enterprise data repositories and reporting systems for proper tracking. There are also software tools offered by CSPs that are useful for risk assessment, threat intelligence feeds, and incident response capabilities. They are used to detect and respond to security incidents in the cloud environment.

- **Vulnerability management:** Cybersecurity often focuses (too much) on identifying and addressing vulnerabilities in IT systems. Vulnerabilities in cloud applications, management software, virtualization platforms, or other components can be exploited by attackers to gain unauthorized access to cloud infrastructure and critical data stores. Regular vulnerability assessments, patching, and secure coding practices are essential to mitigate these risks. Software security practices include conducting regular vulnerability assessments and penetration testing to identify and remediate security weaknesses in these software-based systems. Because cloud infrastructure is available 24/7 and always discoverable by attackers, it is of paramount importance in cloud environments to proactively identify software vulnerabilities and address them before they are exploited.

- **Identity and access management (IAM):** As previously discussed, software plays a significant role in implementing robust IAM policies. This is particularly true within cloud environments. Proper authentication, authorization, and access control mechanisms need to be implemented in software systems provided by the CSPs to ensure that only authorized users and services can access sensitive resources in the cloud. Increasingly, the CSP IAM solutions require substantial software engineering to take advantage of any features beyond the most rudimentary.

- **Authentication and access control:** Cloud security heavily relies on authentication and access control mechanisms to ensure that only authorized users and services can access cloud resources. Software security practices, such as implementing strong authentication mechanisms, enforcing secure password policies, and employing multifactor authentication, help protect against unauthorized access.

- **Secure software development:** Developing secure software is critical to ensuring the integrity and trustworthiness of cloud systems. Secure coding practices, regular security testing, and code reviews help identify and remediate software vulnerabilities early in the development life cycle. Software security measures such as input validation, output encoding, and secure API design are vital to prevent common security vulnerabilities like injection attacks or cross-site scripting (XSS).

- **Virtualization and container security:** Cloud environments often utilize virtualization or containerization technologies to run multiple instances of software. Ensuring the security of these virtualized environments is crucial. Software security measures need to be in place to secure the hypervisors, virtual machines, containers, and container orchestration platforms (all of which are software!) to prevent unauthorized access or escape.

- **Security updates and patch management:** Software security involves keeping software systems up to date with the latest security patches and updates. Cloud environments consist of various software components, including operating systems, databases, and middleware—in addition to the software you deploy to the cloud. Regular updates and patches are essential to address known vulnerabilities and protect against emerging threats.

- **Secure software deployment:** When deploying software in the cloud, it is crucial to ensure that the software components are securely configured and deployed. This includes securely configuring the underlying operating systems, databases, web servers, and application frameworks. Failure to secure these components can lead to vulnerabilities that can be exploited by attackers.

- **Secure APIs and integration:** Cloud environments often involve the integration of multiple software systems and services through application programming interfaces (APIs). Ensuring the security of APIs is crucial to prevent unauthorized access, data leakage, or API abuse that could compromise the cloud environment.

- **Serverless environments:** System developers are spinning up servers where, for the first time ever, they are directly responsible for configuring and considering the deployed environment because the applications are no longer handed off to the IT team before they go live. So in the cloud, software security has a big focus on how it's deployed.

Software is an essential component of cloud security because it specifically embodies the unique challenges and risks associated with the digital transformation that has occurred in cloud computing. The secure development, configuration, and operation of software in the cloud is the only way of ensuring the secure use and protection of data, applications, and infrastructure that run on it. Overall, software security practices and technologies directly impact the security of cloud environments. A holistic approach to cloud security includes robust software security measures throughout the development, deployment, and ongoing management of cloud systems; they are integral to ensuring the security of cloud infrastructure and the security element core to it including IAM, crypto, vulnerability management, intrusion detection, secure APIs, and patch management. Organizations can enhance the overall security posture of their cloud-based systems only by protecting themselves against software born threats and attacks.

Summary

This chapter highlighted the critical importance of software in the realm of cybersecurity. It began by emphasizing how software forms the bedrock of our digital existence, underlining its omnipresence not just in personal devices but also in broader infrastructures such as commerce and communication networks. This pervasiveness has expanded the attack surface for malicious actors, necessitating a more robust commitment to software security.

This chapter underscored software's ubiquitous relevance to cybersecurity, pointing out that it plays a pivotal role in safeguarding sensitive information, critical infrastructure, and personal data. Software is integral across various dimensions of cybersecurity, including prevention, detection, response, and recovery. The evolution of cyber threats, ranging from traditional malware to advanced persistent threats and zero-day exploits, has led to an increased reliance on software as a primary defense line.

Secure communication is another critical aspect, with encryption software and virtual private networks ensuring the safety of digital interactions. Identity and access management systems, crucial for regulating access within networks, are largely software-based and employ methods like multifactor authentication and role-based access control.

The chapter highlighted software-defined security as a transformative concept, enabling organizations to dynamically adapt their security measures. This approach includes software-defined networks and perimeters that segment networks, enhancing resilience against attacks.

This chapter also discussed the role of software in proactive cybersecurity approaches, such as threat hunting, using advanced analytics and algorithms for early detection of compromises. It further delved into the importance of software in training and awareness programs, emphasizing the need for role-based training for technical development teams.

In incident response and recovery, software-driven platforms are indispensable for assessing breaches, coordinating remediation efforts, and ensuring data recovery. The evolving digital landscape makes the role of software in cybersecurity more significant, driving innovation and shaping the future of secure digital interactions.

The chapter also explored artificial intelligence in cybersecurity. It highlighted AI's potential to revolutionize threat detection, automate incident response, and enhance malware detection and behavioral analysis. However, there are also challenges and ethical considerations of AI, including privacy concerns and the risk of bias and discrimination.

The final section of the chapter integrated cloud security with software security, considering cloud security as a subset of overall software security. It covered various aspects, including encryption and data protection; application security; infrastructure as code (IaC); software-powered governance, risk, and compliance; and vulnerability management in cloud environments. The chapter argued that the secure development, configuration, and operation of software in the cloud are essential for protecting data, applications, and infrastructure.

In this chapter, I endeavored to stress the inextricable link between software and cybersecurity, urging job seekers and professionals in the field to understand how software functions and fails to better evaluate and mitigate software risks.

Chapter 7

The Power of Diversity and Inclusion in Cybersecurity: Safeguarding the Digital Frontier

It's an interconnected world, and cyber threats loom large. Those threats take on many forms from a wide variety of peoples. They're a diverse bunch and, as a result, quite creative in their approaches to the offensive security that make them a threat. To defend against this army of malice, you need an equally diverse talent pool. Unfortunately, we are far from that desired state at present.

In November 2022, The Ponemon Institute released a study titled "Achieving Diversity in the U.S. Cybersecurity Industry." It outlined an approach to increase diversity talent pools across the United States and highlighted where we, as a country and an industry, are falling short today. The Ponemon Institute surveyed 3,870 individuals in the United States who are cybersecurity practitioners about the state of diversity in their organizations. I discuss some of those findings later in this chapter; however, first, I define what I mean by diversity in cyber and then talk about some of the benefits of adopting a proactive diversity and inclusion (D&I) initiative as a critical part of a successful cybersecurity strategy.

The significance of diversity and inclusion in cybersecurity cannot be overstated. Diversity and inclusion encompass more than just gender and ethnicity; they embrace a multitude of perspectives, experiences, and backgrounds. By fostering a diverse and inclusive workforce, the cybersecurity industry not only strengthens its defense against evolving threats but also nurtures innovation and growth. Let's explore my definition of diversity and inclusion in cybersecurity, explore some of the benefits they bring, and highlight the potential consequences of a homogeneous workforce.

Defining Diversity and Inclusion in Cybersecurity

When I talk about *diversity* in cybersecurity, I refer to the representation of individuals from various demographics, such as race, gender, age, sexual orientation, disability, education, work experience, and cultural background. This definition encompasses a wide range of skills, experiences, and perspectives. Inclusion, on the other hand, focuses on creating an environment where diverse individuals feel valued, respected, and empowered to contribute their unique insights for the betterment of the team or mission as a whole.

In the context of cybersecurity, diversity and inclusion are crucial for building effective defense mechanisms against ever-evolving threats. By assembling teams with diverse skill sets and backgrounds, organizations can better understand and anticipate attackers' tactics. Diverse perspectives foster creative problem-solving, enabling teams to develop innovative strategies to combat cyber threats.

Some Benefits of Diversity and Inclusion in Cybersecurity

Enhanced problem-solving, improved decision-making, and heightened innovation and creativity are just some of the business benefits of cyber D&I. According to several published research studies from reputable firms, diversity has positive cultural and business benefits. At the 2021 Global PCI Community Meeting, I had the great pleasure of co-presenting with my friend, Sherron Burgess, an accomplished CISO and diversity ambassador. This was a follow-on presentation to the ones I delivered in 2019 in the United States and Europe at the PCI Community Meetings. Sherron and I offered practical tips on how to attract, recruit, retain, and develop diverse cyber talent; we also referenced some previously published studies about the benefits of doing so.

- *Harvard Business Review*
  - Diverse teams are able to solve problems faster than cognitively similar people.
- McKinsey's research
  - Gender-diverse companies are 15 percent more likely to outperform their peers.
  - Ethnically diverse companies are 35 percent more likely to do the same.
- Catalyst research
  - Companies with more women on the board statistically outperform peers.
- Deloitte research
  - Inclusive teams outperform their peers by 80 percent in team-based assessments.
  - Engagement is an outcome of diversity and inclusion.

Diverse teams bring a wider range of perspectives, experiences, and expertise to the table. This diversity of thought fosters more robust problem-solving approaches, as team members can draw upon their unique insights and knowledge. By combining different viewpoints, teams can identify vulnerabilities and devise effective countermeasures that a homogeneous team may overlook.

Inclusive environments empower individuals to contribute their opinions without fear of judgment or exclusion. This psychological safety encourages open and honest communication, allowing diverse teams to engage in constructive debates and make more informed decisions. Diverse perspectives challenge groupthink, reduce biases, and lead to more effective risk assessment and mitigation strategies.

Diversity in cybersecurity drives innovation by encouraging fresh ideas and creative thinking. When individuals from different backgrounds collaborate, they bring a multitude of experiences and approaches to problem-solving. This amalgamation of ideas leads to novel solutions and strategies, enabling organizations to stay ahead in the cat-and-mouse game with cyber criminals.

Knowing these benefits, you also have the unique opportunity to tap into and create a broader talent pool by embracing diversity. Doing so expands the talent pool for cybersecurity organizations. By fostering an inclusive environment, organizations attract individuals from diverse backgrounds who may have previously been discouraged from entering the field. This widens the pool of skilled professionals, helping to address the industry's persistent talent shortage.

Imagine if you could solve multiple problems facing the cybersecurity industry at the same time.

- Shortage of skilled talent
- Millions of unfilled jobs around the world
- Lack of diversity

You can. I'll discuss more about this shortly.

Drawbacks and Dangers of Homogeneous Workforces

A homogeneous workforce in cybersecurity can have far-reaching implications that hinder progress and undermine security. Limited perspectives result in a restricted range of approaches and creativity. Homogeneous teams are more likely to develop blind spots, miss emerging threats, and fail to understand the motivations of diverse attacker profiles. This restricted worldview can create vulnerabilities that adversaries exploit, jeopardizing the security of systems and data.

We all have unconscious biases that taint us. A homogeneous workforce is even more susceptible to unconscious biases that can hinder effective decision-making and perpetuate existing inequalities. Biases can lead to overlooking the potential of talented individuals, creating an environment of exclusion and stifling the industry's growth. This can make teams struggle to generate new ideas due to the absence of diverse insights and experiences. Without fresh perspectives challenging the status quo, organizations may become stagnant and fail to adapt to rapidly evolving cyber threats.

Cybersecurity is a global issue, and understanding diverse cultural contexts is critical for effective defense. A workforce with limited cultural competency lacks the ability to respond appropriately to threats that may vary across regions or communities, leaving organizations ill-prepared to protect against targeted attacks.

Diversity and inclusion are not just buzzwords in the cybersecurity industry; they are fundamental pillars for building robust defense mechanisms. Embracing diversity and fostering inclusion cultivates in an environment of innovation, creativity, and improved decision-making. By bringing together individuals with different backgrounds and perspectives, organizations can better understand and combat the ever-evolving landscape of cyber threats. It is imperative that the cybersecurity industry continues to champion diversity and inclusion, recognizing that only by working together can we safeguard the digital frontier and protect the systems and data that underpin our modern world.

Underrepresentation in the Cybersecurity Industry

Gender disparity remains a significant issue in the cybersecurity industry. While progress has been made, women continue to be underrepresented in cybersecurity roles. According to the November 2022 Ponemon research previously mentioned, the cybersecurity profession is dominated by males, with only 18 percent of 3,870 respondents identifying as female. Other studies from the Aspen Institute and the International Information System Security Certification Consortium (ISC2) reported slightly higher numbers in earlier years; however, all of the studies show that women in cybersecurity represent significantly lesser percentages than they do in the U.S. workforce overall, which is 56.8 percent according to the U.S. Bureau of Labor and Statistics from 2022.

The gender gap is even more pronounced in leadership positions, where women occupy a mere 9–13 percent of executive-level roles. This lack of representation at the top perpetuates a cycle of exclusion, limiting opportunities for women to contribute to decision-making, innovation, and policy development within the industry.

In addition to gender disparity, the cybersecurity industry grapples with significant racial and ethnic underrepresentation. The lack of diversity within the industry is evident across various ethnic groups. For instance, the number of people identifying as Black, Hispanic, and Native American remains underrepresented, making up a small fraction of the cybersecurity workforce: 9 percent, 4 percent, and 1 percent, respectively. The more recent Ponemon data similarly placed Blacks at 12 percent, Asians at 8 percent, and Native Americans at 1 percent. As you can see in Figure 7.1, those who identify as Black, Hispanic, and American Indian are dramatically underrepresented in the cybersecurity workforce compared to their distribution among the U.S. population.

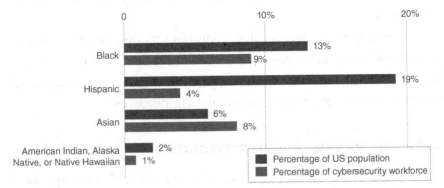

Figure 7.1   Racial and ethnic diversity in the cybersecurity workforce
Data courtesy of Ponemon Institute

Intersectionality and Multiple Marginalized Identities

Addressing underrepresentation in the cybersecurity industry must involve an understanding of intersectionality, which recognizes that individuals possess multiple marginalized identities that can compound their experiences of discrimination. Intersectionality emphasizes the importance of considering gender, race, ethnicity, and other factors simultaneously, as individuals with intersecting identities face unique barriers and biases. For example, women of color face both gender and racial discrimination, which exacerbates the challenges they encounter in entering and advancing in the cybersecurity field. Intersectionality also highlights the need for tailored approaches to promote diversity and inclusion, acknowledging that a one-size-fits-all solution is woefully insufficient.

It is this very lack of diversity that prevents us from building and attracting a wider talent pool to bridge the significant skills gap that currently exists. We need a more robust workforce that can better safeguard digital infrastructures, and we have the means to achieve it by taking advantage of existing assets, applying the diligence to methodically build D&I programs, and making a focused commitment to do so.

There are many factors that contribute to underrepresentation in cybersecurity, including stereotypes and biases (conscious and unconscious), lack of role models and mentors, educational barriers, and uninformed organizational recruitment practices.

Efforts to Address Underrepresentation

To address underrepresentation in the cybersecurity industry, concerted efforts are required at multiple levels. First, educational institutions and training programs should promote cybersecurity education and awareness among underrepresented groups, encouraging young individuals from diverse backgrounds to pursue careers in the field. One way into cybersecurity is to enroll in college and graduate with a degree in cybersecurity.

According to the U.S. Bureau of Labor Statistics, people with a college degree earn about 67 percent more than those whose highest qualification is a high school diploma. Given the social and economic barriers that minorities face, college is often not an option. However, some historically black colleges and universities (HBCUs) have created places to establish a pipeline for underrepresented minorities into the cybersecurity workforce through academic offerings, like Shaw University's Center for Cybersecurity Education and Research. Similarly, Hispanic Serving Institutions (HSIs) like Pueblo Community College offer certificate programs in cyber defense, computer forensics, and information assurance basic. These higher education institutions need help from industry partners to attract more students who can afford these valuable programs.

Government initiatives and policies can also play a crucial role in addressing underrepresentation, such as providing funding for scholarships and grants that support diverse students pursuing cybersecurity education. Collaboration between industry leaders, academia, and government agencies is essential to drive meaningful change and achieve greater representation within the cybersecurity sector.

In July 2023, the Biden-Harris administration in the U.S. White House announced its *National Cyber Workforce and Education Strategy*, which they subtitled "Unleashing America's Cyber Talent." The measures outlined by the White House are commendable, and the investments committed are mostly to solid organizations that will produce useful programs. However, the lack of skilled professionals for cybersecurity jobs is exacerbated by the very companies that complain about the lack of talent. Until managers, executives, and HR professionals in cybersecurity-hiring positions create realistic job descriptions and accept the fact that *entry level* means "no previous paid professional experience," we will never progress.

Take, for example, the analysis of 10,584 entry-level cybersecurity jobs conducted by AccessCyber in 2023. Seventy-one percent of those "entry-level" jobs listed some experience required. Some offer equivalency for unpaid internships and online training courses, but that is often buried and never seen by would-be applicants turned off by the unseemly paradox.

There are some bright spots and opportunities to make a transformational change in both the cybersecurity industry and many people's lives. Here are a few tips, supported by that same research from AccessCyber:

- Encourage employees and would-be hires to obtain industry certifications. Eighty-three percent of those 10,584 entry-level cybersecurity jobs list an industry certification as a desired skill/competency.

Beware HR and hiring managers: CISSP might be the most popular cybersecurity certification, but it requires *five years* of experience to qualify even to just sit for the exam. Companies need to stop listing this certification on entry-level job descriptions.

- Ninety-two percent of entry-level cybersecurity job descriptions asked candidates to be familiar with "frameworks, standards, and regulations" like PCI-DSS, HIPAA, GDPR, NIST Cybersecurity Framework, and ISO 27000.
- Less than 24 percent of jobs require an undergraduate degree.

Based on these three bullet points (certifications, frameworks, and four-year degree not required), there is a formula that companies and individuals alike can follow to help create net-new cybersecurity professionals. Get trained on a specific cybersecurity framework and obtain at least one industry certification to become a much more attractive/hirable candidate. Imagine if we can further solve the lack of diversity problem facing the cybersecurity industry at the same time.

As discussed earlier in this chapter, D&I is proven to make good business sense as well as have positive social and economic impacts. How do we address the lack of talent and diversity issues simultaneously? Organizations and individuals can solicit the help of organizations like Cyversity (www.cyversity.org), WiCyS (www.wicys.org), and others that have programming aimed specifically at under-represented demographic groups like women, people of color, the LGBTQ+ community, veterans, and others. These groups all offer excellent training and mentorship programs, mainly directly aligned to the very frameworks, standards, and certifications coveted by hiring managers.

As leaders in the cybersecurity industry, we can partner with these nonprofits, encourage our team members to join and get involved with the programs they offer, and use the jobs boards as a recruiting platform. These organizations offer internships, training, mentor programs, job and résumé preparation workshops, conferences with job fairs, and other excellent programming that addresses the exact problems we need solved for cyber talent. Forward-thinking companies like Google, Target, United Airlines, Workday, Mass Mutual, and others are sponsors that invest money in these nonprofits so they can build and execute the programs they offer. In addition to being a source of new talent, Cyversity, WiCyS, and others are also excellent places for your current teams to get re-skilled and upskilled in cybersecurity.

For individuals, employers will want to see that you can be self-taught, are networked, and are open to learning new things. In Chapter 8, I share feedback from cybersecurity practitioners I interviewed as part of the research for this book. I spoke to 150 different people and captured their thoughts, recommendations, and preferences when it comes to addressing the cybersecurity skills shortage and D&I challenges. I touch upon some of the latter in the following section of this chapter, but the career advice from these experts follows in more detail in Chapter 8.

One thing for both hiring managers and job seekers to keep in mind is that industry certifications are particularly powerful. As mentioned, 83 percent of those 10,584 entry-level cybersecurity jobs analyzed by AccessCyber list an industry certification as a desired skill. Additionally, of the 3,870 cybersecurity professionals surveyed in the

The Power of Diversity and Inclusion in Cybersecurity

aforementioned Ponemon research, 75 percent of them have at least one certification, and 17 percent had four or more.

I mentioned that I delivered very well-received presentations at PCI Community Meetings (the global conferences put on by the PCI Council); I also did the same at the annual NICE conference (put on by NIST). The later versions of those presentations were titled "DIY D&I with PCI" and outlined precisely the same cookbook strategy I write about previously.

> *Combine a framework/standard (like PCI-DSS) with the steeply discounted and sometimes free training available from the likes of Cyversity (and others), and we can resolve both the diversity and lack of talent problems at the same time.*

These presentations were the second-highest rated talks of the PCI conferences, bested only by the keynote given by the NASA astronaut who showed pictures and videos from his spacewalk as he repaired the Hubble telescope (the talk had little to do with cybersecurity, but it was a tough act to follow nevertheless!).

Achieving Diversity in the U.S. Cybersecurity Industry

I want to dive deeper into that November 2022 Ponemon Institute research. There is a lot to unpack in there, and I asked a number of cybersecurity leaders to help me analyze and comment on that report. I find their insights useful, and I think others will too. Later in this chapter, I discuss some case studies of how a few leaders built successful D&I programs. I also highlight the journey of one particular individual whose life was transformed by efforts born of D&I. But first, the Ponemon research.

Addressing the Age Gap

We talk a lot about the lack of gender and race diversity in cyber-security; however, one area that often goes overlooked is age. The Ponemon report discovered that "cybersecurity is a young profession" with 60 percent of respondents younger than 40. I asked a leader at Google what they thought about this and how we could encourage and attract midcareer transitions into cybersecurity. Here is the response:

> To solve the cybersecurity talent gap, we need to focus not only on the current generation that is joining the work-force, but also those with related experiences, skills, and an interest in cybersecurity. We can do this by creating clear pathways and opportunities, such as condensed training programs, on-the-job development, and self-learning experiences. This will enable those not enrolled in full-time degree programs to explore cybersecurity opportunities and apply their past experiences while bringing a new diverse lens of thinking to the field.

You'll note a similar pattern: focused training and self-learn opportunities building on existing skills with cyber-specific education. This leader talked about military veterans, another demographic not heavily represented in cyber, as a fertile and under-tapped pool of mature talent we should focus on as an industry.

Aligning the Expectations

I asked my friend Sherron Burgess to comment on another finding from the Ponemon research, specifically, this finding, "To improve diversity in the workforce, organizations should ensure job candidates understand the expectations they have when hiring." As a CISO,

I wanted to hear her perspective on this finding and inquire about what hiring organizations can do to ensure their job descriptions and expectations are reasonable. This is what she said:

> It is vital for hiring managers, recruiters, and organizations to align their job descriptions to skills and capabilities sought in candidates. Far too often, job descriptions are cookie-cutter and require skills that are not aligned to the level of resource sought (i.e., entry-level position with CISSP). This disconnected approach taken by organizations tends to eliminate diverse populations who often times will not apply out of concern that they cannot meet the qualifications and expectations of the role. To course correct, it is critical that organizations understand, prioritize, and evaluate the critical skills that candidates need walking in the door (e.g., critical thinking, growth mindset, willingness to learn) and tailor their job descriptions and candidate pools accordingly.

Increasing Retention Rate

Another critical finding of this ground-breaking research was that people do not last long in jobs. This is particularly true of earlier-stage professionals. The Ponemon report found "most respondents have been in their current position less than three years, indicating a high rate of turnover." Retention of talent is key, so I asked another experienced cybersecurity professional and educator what organizations can do to stem the migration to other jobs and/or professions. Beverly Benson answered that organizations can retain talent simply by fostering an inclusive environment where employees are encouraged to share both their ideas and concerns. She said it was this simple step, coupled with the necessity of organizations also ensuring that compensation packages remain competitive to the marketplace, is the key to talent retention.

An Open Discussion About Cybersecurity Diversity

As part of my Ed TALKS show (`www.edtalks.io`), I had the pleasure of discussing the Ponemon report and cybersecurity diversity in-depth with Dr. Larry Ponemon himself, alongside Devon Bryan, a long-time industry veteran C-level executive and cofounder of Cyversity, and Sarah Morales, the lead for Google's cybersecurity community engagement programs. The video recording of this hour-long discussion can be found at the previous URL and is titled "Diversity & Inclusion in Cybersecurity – Reaping the Rewards." I summarize some of those highlights here, because I find them particularly helpful to both underrepresented individuals who want to begin their cyber journey and organizations that want to make a genuine commitment to diversity and inclusion in cybersecurity.

The inability to retain a diverse cybersecurity workforce is making it difficult to close the diversity gap. In fact, 63 percent of respondents cited this as the main block to closing the gap, ahead of both limited budgets and support from senior leadership. Devon Bryan, who is one of those senior leaders, had two pieces of advice.

> If organizations hiring execs within the cyber field would be more aggressive and think more outside the box in terms of upskilling, and re-skilling existing practitioners, we might not have this huge gap that we do have in unfilled jobs within cyber.

> Leaders must have the courage to stand up for what they believe in. If D&I is important to you, are you going

The Power of Diversity and Inclusion in Cybersecurity

to have the courage to take a stance and the integrity to drive initiatives that could potentially cause friction across the organization and push back? Organizations and leaders whom I admire in this space have demonstrated both those qualities. They walk the talk and demonstrate courage in tackling what is a very difficult issue, and they have moved forward on those with tangible outcomes.

Sarah Morales of Google offered other advice.

I think coaching and support are really important. People get in the door and then sometimes, especially in big organizations, can feel a little lost or feel sometimes like the only woman or the only person of color in the room. Invest in programs like mentorship and sponsorship. Give people the opportunities to meet senior leaders who might have similar identities or allies of different identities. Give space for people to lead projects and propose new ideas. "Stretch opportunities" is a big thing within Google's culture—giving people those chances and having safe spaces for them if they fail. If they can't reach their stretch goal, they need to be able to learn from that and still be supported by their managers. Stretch opportunities build trust in management. Trust leads to retention.

Dr. Ponemon pointed out that people in cybersecurity careers want to stay there. Seventy-four percent said they are likely or very likely to stay in the cybersecurity profession the next two to four years. This is probably because the pay is very good—83 percent of those surveyed reported that salary and benefits are adequate (fair) or more than adequate. However, Dr. Ponemon warned that the lack of D&I is generating some troubling signs that could disrupt that satisfaction and intent on staying in the field.

Eighty percent of cybersecurity professionals told us diversity is important to them; yet, only 39 percent of those same professionals feel they presently work in a diverse cybersecurity workforce. These counter-pressures cannot coexist for very long. Couple this data with the fact that 59 percent of respondents say it is "not likely" or there is "no chance" that the D&I gap will shrink in the next two to four years, and I think we've got a real problem brewing.

The summary of this research report was well written and collated with other data collected by the Ponemon Institute over the years. It reads, and I summarize, that a challenge most organizations have in trying to achieve a strong cybersecurity posture is the ability to hire and retain skilled cybersecurity professionals. This recognition should encourage more organizations to take such steps to improve diversity and inclusion, specifically the following:

- Establishing cybersecurity apprenticeship programs
- Allocating resources to fund organizations' efforts to develop cybersecurity diversity programs
- Providing financial support to cover the costs of certification programs

It is also important to start outreach early. Organizations should encourage high schools and community colleges to invite cybersecurity practitioners to speak to and mentor students about cybersecurity career opportunities with a particular focus on underrepresented communities and the education institutions that serve those groups.

Promoting Inclusive Hiring Practices and Encouraging Educational Pathways

Organizations such as Accenture, Google, and others have dropped their four-year college requirement for cybersecurity jobs. This helps the enterprise and the underrepresented alike. Less formal education, such as two-year degree programs, industry certifications, a strong work ethic, and willingness to learn, are increasingly coveted characteristics for entry-level positions. Many organizations work with local security and technology groups, conferences, and so on. As a cybersecurity job seeker, get yourself out there to be seen and network. As hiring managers, participate in or sponsor these local groups and events to broadcast your interest.

I've even seen companies send nonsecurity staff to security conferences to learn—people from procurement, finance, and legal who later ended up in cybersecurity functions or become security champions for their functional groups. These creative educational pathways are highly effective and can foster the trust in leadership that Sarah Morales of Google mentioned when commenting on the Ponemon study.

Organizations can also augment flexibility in interview processes and/or work schedules. For example, when recruiting for penetration test engineers, my company posts a job description that has been reviewed internally, carefully scrubbed of insensitive/dated terminology, and meticulously analyzed for appropriate requirements displayed to applicants. When an applicant applies for the job, they receive a single URL in response. It is a challenge site, a capture-the-flag type of website that gives them a specific task and puzzle to solve. If they complete the task, they are directed to a second challenge site that is more difficult, and they're given a time-boxed mission: find as many security vulnerabilities as you can in the next 72 hours and send us a report detailing which vulnerabilities you found and, for each one, how you found it, the steps to reproduce it, your estimate of potential impact/severity, and a suggestion for how to remediate it.

In this mission, we are testing not only their technical acumen but their time management ability, their writing and communication skills, and their ability to articulate both red team (attack/offensive) and blue team (remediation/defensive) competency. If we like what we see when we read the report, we pretty much already know we want to hire the candidate. Yet, we do not yet know their name, race, sex, creed, color, religious preference, and so on. This helps remove unconscious biases from our hiring process. We know we'd like to hire the candidate and only then do we schedule a live discussion. These are the types of steps that organizations can take to help promote inclusive hiring practices in cybersecurity.

Another colleague of mine mentioned a lesson she learned during the COVID-19 pandemic, when many companies realized that remote working and home offices can be just as effective for certain job functions. She had met a woman who was a longtime researcher in cybersecurity. The lady said one of the things that her company did was allow her when she had children to work part-time. This allowed her to stay in the workforce. She was able to work part-time, from a different location, and that kept her active in the field. Today, this woman is a very well-known cyber speaker and luminary; she has a number of patents and many referenced research studies with her name on them. That flexibility that her employer allowed (well before the COVID-19 pandemic) kept her in the industry and helped make her the cybersecurity superstar she is today. Supporting that kind of flexibility is another way that many companies have learned to retain cyber talent.

As an individual looking for opportunities in cybersecurity, take inspiration from this part-time worker. Are you particularly passionate about an area of cybersecurity? Maybe find a part of this huge industry that you care about. Whether it is detection response or red teaming or compliance ... zero day exploits, research, artificial intelligence, the cloud, IoT, cybercrime investigation, fraud analysis ... whatever. Figure out what you enjoy most and dive deeply into that. But there are also those long-term big issues, like Internet standards and security frameworks, that keep moving along and are in high demand. You can dive into those too and find a lucrative career for yourself in cybersecurity.

Case Studies: Successful Diversity and Inclusion Programs

Creating a more diverse security workforce requires collaboration among the entire ecosystem.

- **Individuals:** Motivated to learn, ambitious, and willing to put in the effort.

- **Corporations and government:** Investing in programs to attract, hire, develop, and retain diverse cybersecurity talent. This includes the recruiting process, career pathing, job description roles and responsibilities, and so on.

- **Nonprofit organizations and communities:** Committed to achieving more consistent representation of women, underrepresented minorities, veterans, and so on, in the cybersecurity industry via education, mentorship, networking, and access to organizations that want to hire its members.

Many nonprofits organize community events for networking, but often these same nonprofits lack training or skill-building expertise. Having strategic partners to fill those gaps, in addition to sponsors willing to help fund program development, is a critical element for success. The three groups are co-dependent to help underrepresented demographics gain skills but also take their cybersecurity career progress to the next level by connecting those interested in cyber jobs with mentors and enterprises, thus giving them access to interviews and opportunities to connect with hiring managers. While the industry works on improving its hiring practices, the programs co-created by nonprofits, government, and industry can serve as a conduit to get diverse talent "invited to the dance" and help accelerate this goal of driving more underrepresented populations into the workforce.

I am first going to highlight a couple of brief case studies from leaders I've worked with over the past five or so years. These folks have either built, overseen, or witnessed diversity and inclusion efforts in cybersecurity—some successful and some not so successful. We can learn from all of it. I then follow these case studies with a longer one that follows the path of a single individual over the course of several years. I hope you find all of these case studies interesting and useful to your own journey.

Case Study 1: Do It with Love

Edna Conway is one of my all-time favorites. She is an inspirational leader, a remarkably intelligent and personable human being, and her capacity for conceiving of and then systematically executing solutions to absolutely massive problems is nothing short of spectacular. I first met Ed (as she prefers to be called) when she was serving as chief security officer for Cisco's Global Value Chain, which included its Supply Chain Operations, Worldwide Partner Channel, and Technical Services Organizations. She was the executive responsible for developing, leading, and delivering the company's strategy to assess, monitor, and continuously improve security and resilience for all things (physical and digital) that constituted the Cisco supply chain. She later went on to a similar role with Microsoft Azure.

Edna and I briefly served together on the board of directors at Cyversity; however, it was her educational background that drew me to her initially. Her undergraduate degree is in medieval and renaissance literature, after which she went to law school. I also have an undergraduate degree in literature and ended up in cybersecurity. Those similarities and our joint interest in diversity and inclusion made for instant friends. Ed and I were supposed to jointly present a talk at the 2019 PCI North American Community Meeting titled "Opening the Talent Spigot to Secure Our Digital Future," but she was called away on an urgent business matter days before the event, so instead I interviewed her and made her story one of the case studies presented at that conference.

Ed thinks big. She grounds her lofty vision with practical, deliberate tactics. This may be one of the keys to her success. I call it *helicopter vision*; the ability to soar high and see far and wide coupled with the ability to dive low and visualize the discrete steps needed to walk the path to succeed. She has a simple philosophy when it comes to success in cyber D&I.

- Start early.
- Integrate versus invent.
- Consolidate for scale.

Ed says there is a need for education at multiple levels, starting with teen and pre-teenaged children. She thinks pre-college STEM initiatives that target middle school digital natives—such as the Girl Scouts' cyber badge program—are a great place to start. "I spend my time with 8 and 10-year-olds because I think we need to get to them early—you need to get them before hormones kick in quite frankly."

She urged parents and teachers to look for and encourage signs of interest, "If it's in your blood, it's in your blood. If you see a young girl playing with an Erector Set, you should think, 'There's a mechanical engineer in the making.'" Just when virtual-Edna is sitting on the ground building trusses with that 10-year-old girl, her helicopter vision kicks in, and she's reminded of things like gender bias and the many careers in cyber that don't require STEM backgrounds.

"We also have an obligation to open our minds to the existing members of the workforce who are sociologists, economics experts, actuaries—folks who can think about risk, who have different talents, and bring them in. Because we will not meet our cybersecurity staffing needs if we do not take *today's* workforce and embrace the capabilities they have."

Ed even suggested that IT departments resurrect the concept of "juried craftspeople" where apprentices are taken in by a craftsperson to learn the "CyberCraft." After all, she herself is the quintessential embodiment of that kind of on-the-job learning and diversity. With an origin in Renaissance literature that evolved into law, she developed herself into a preeminent leader in cybersecurity supply chain resilience. "Guess what, we can learn," she concluded. As you'll see in the research results presented in the next chapter, the willingness and ability to always learn is a highly prized attribute when managers look to hire cybersecurity talent.

Ed also recommends embedding security into existing programs that already have success introducing new concepts to receptive audiences. She brought up FIRST (www.firstinspires.org) as an example of such a program. Her philosophy is that these organizations have a captive audience in their membership already committed to learning

The Power of Diversity and Inclusion in Cybersecurity

something new. They have programs and infrastructure to leverage. Rather than trying to re-create all of this, partner with them to help them integrate cybersecurity.

Building on that last point, Ed astutely observed that there are many organizations trying to solve the same or similar problems. This is a topic she discussed at Cyversity board meetings. Ed suggested the concept of a "community garden of cybersecurity D&I" where various nonprofit organizations specialize in a particular area or demographic. What was missing, in her opinion, was the glue that could bridge these organizations and offer an assembly line where each station does its work and then transitions to the next station. Ed admits this is a lofty goal that will take some focus and funding, but her point remains—there are many grassroot efforts that could combine efforts to gain economies of scale and grab a significant amount of attention (and funding) from large enterprises who want to make a global impact.

Ed's parting advice to any person, group, or enterprise interested in making a change in cybersecurity diversity and inclusion: "Do it with love. Do it because you care." In the most poignant example of her helicopter vision, she said, "Choose to help just one person—just one—and watch the ripples."

Case Study 2: Remove the Intimidation Factor

I met Vandana Verma at a conference in Bengaluru in 2018. At the time, she introduced herself as the OWASP Bangalore Chapter Leader. Little did I know how ambitious, passionate, impactful, and impressive her efforts were around the globe to encourage women and young adults to learn about cybersecurity. Among the many things that Vandana has accomplished and continues to do are the following:

- Several years on the OWASP global board of directors promoting open-source security standards and best practices

- Frequent speaker, trainer, and mentor at global conferences, such as Black Hat, RSA, Global AppSec, Grace Hopper, and BSides
- Multiple award winner for leadership, influence, and innovation in cybersecurity
- And my personal favorite: influential advocate for diversity and inclusion in cybersecurity, aiming to inspire, educate, and empower the next generation of security professionals

Regarding diversity and inclusion, Vandana founded, leads, and supports various programs such as InfoSec Girls, WoSec, and Infosec Kids. She initially stood up for InfoSec Girls in India to remove the intimidation barriers she experienced herself as a female security engineer. InfoSec Girls delivers free training to young females, taught by women for women. She also spends time each year delivering free training at the OWASP Seaside (and other) conferences to all diversity groups (third gender, any religion, whatever). She does this to make both a personal and professional impact, to encourage continual dialogue, and to remove obstacles, primarily knowledge. She believes that knowledge is the spark that can launch someone into a cybersecurity career. She wants women and other underrepresented groups to at least have the chance to learn in a safe, nonintimidating place. Vandana was fortunate to have a mentor who exposed her to information security at an impressionable age. She wants to pass this along with a focus on young people and women.

One strategy Vandana employs during her training initiatives is to take advantage of pervasive and de facto standards such as PCI-DSS and OWASP Top 10. She said these have been a great door opener for women and minorities, especially in audit work roles, where one does not need to necessarily be technical to obtain a good-paying cybersecurity job. During her training sessions she reminds her students that because these standards are often mandatory, it "gives them teeth" and keeps security top of mind as a driving function.

She also reminds students that even though they may be auditing technical groups, like software development and IT teams, those groups are unlikely to know security—so don't be intimidated. Their job, as security auditors, is to illuminate the security controls and best practices and then seek validation that an acceptable level of due diligence has been performed or an acceptable compensating control has been put in place. Vandana views standards like PCI-DSS and OWAS Top 10 as a huge opportunity for minorities to get into cybersecurity. "Most companies need to comply, so why not learn about these standards? It can only help you," She noted.

When asked to provide advice to organizations that want to improve diversity and inclusion initiatives, Vandana's answer is twofold.

- **Focus on niche sectors, for example, law and psychology, as a source for cyber talent:** Leverage their baseline skills and augment their knowledge with areas needed at your company specific to cybersecurity. There is a need for differentiation, so this strategy can help in multiple ways.

- **Remove groupthink:** Encourage individual contribution from each person. The bane of cybersecurity teams, in Vandana's opinion, is "playing follow the leader blindly over the cliff," and the best path toward success includes proactively reaching out to solicit various ideas about a particularly vexing security problem. "Diversity fosters creativity, which in turn, fosters aha moments," she told me.

Case Study 3: Ghanaian Grit

This is a story about Joshua Berkoh. I first read Joshua's name on a list of people who had applied for a training scholarship offered by

Cyversity. It was March 2021, and the nonprofit had recently received sponsorship funding from Google and decided to offer free training for 200 members, split into two cohorts: red team and blue team. Cyversity and Google brought in two training partners to deliver the training to the 200 members: Security Innovation and Range Force. Of the 200 chosen for the scholarship, 142 opted for red team training and 58 for blue team. Joshua was part of the red team cohort and the only person from West Africa selected for the scholarship. At the time, he was unemployed and approaching one year after graduation from his undergraduate university program.

The training was an intensive six-month agenda broken into two phases: initial online and instructor-led training on cybersecurity fundamentals and specific red and blue team skills development. Most of the hands-on learning happened on live cyber ranges the training providers included as part of their curricula. Both Security Innovation and Range Force donated 100 percent of the training courses, cyber range access, and instructors to this Cyversity/Google initiative. After the first three months of training, Google hosted private information sessions for the students to discuss "a day in the life" of a red teamer or blue teamer at Google. These sessions gave students a glimpse into what a job in one of these primary color slices is like at one of the world's preeminent technology companies. Students were then paired with mentors and offered free résumé writing and mock interview workshops during the second three-month training cycle, which focused more on advanced topics in red/blue teaming. At the end of the six-month program, students were encouraged to apply for entry-level jobs on the Cyversity jobs board. Figure 7.2 shows a brief infographic of the training track and a couple of quotes from participants.

Back to Joshua. His training was challenging. He lived in his family home at the time with his parents and siblings. He would wait until everyone was asleep at night to take his training so he could connect his laptop to the one television the family had. This larger screen helped him have both the training material and the cyber practice range visible at the same time so he could easily toggle between the two. Joshua was one of the 89 people who completed all of the requirements of the red team program (only 62 percent made it all the way through). He participated in as many Cyversity activities as he could. By the time he finished the program in September, he was applying for jobs in Ghana. He got one. Some people would be satisfied there, but the fire was lit in Joshua.

He performed well at his job but also took the initiative to apply to graduate school in the United States. By early spring of 2022, Joshua received an offer from the University of Cincinnati to enroll in the cybersecurity graduate program. They offered him a paid teaching assistant (TA) role and assistance with living accommodations. This unemployed Ghanaian who had never left his country nor ever flown in an airplane was headed for America!

But Joshua's story does not end there. After achieving a perfect 4.0 GPA in his first graduate year at the University of Cincinnati, he obtained a lucrative internship at Intuit. The company paid Joshua well and even paid for a luxury apartment and all travel costs for this three-month internship. As of the writing of this book, Joshua is in the second year of his graduate program and maintains a 4.0 GPA.

Now, for the rest of the story. Joshua is not only an intelligent, hard-working young man; he is also committed to giving back to those in need. The Cyversity scholarship lit another fire in Joshua. He wanted to help other Ghanaians who, like him, are intelligent, hard-working, and looking for a chance to earn a good-paying job. He fought his natural shyness and tracked down the CEO of Security Innovation, the training partner of Google and Cyversity that put him through six months of free red team training. He wanted to see if that CEO would be willing to assist Joshua in his mission to enable other cybersecurity newbies in Ghana. I am that CEO.

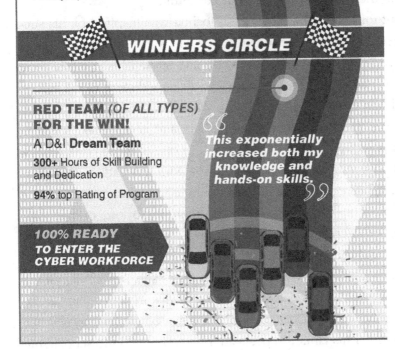

THE FAST TRACK
LAMOTH ONLY 3 MONTHS TO FINISH LINE

GETTING UP TO SPEED
26 Cources:
Basics, OWASP, Testing,
Pen Testing

PITSHOP
Live hacking, expert
instructors, 24x7 support on
orld-renowned cyber range
to buils on learned skills.

**ACCELERATE TO THE
FINISH LINE**
20 Advanced Courses:
Red Team and Scanning OWASP
Advanced, Advanced Pen
Testing, Specialized Pen Testing

As a Black Transman, looking forward to how this organization progresses diversity in this field.

WINNERS CIRCLE

RED TEAM (OF ALL TYPES) FOR THE WIN!

A D&I **Dream Team**

300+ Hours of Skill Building
and Dedication

94% top Rating of Program

This exponentially increased both my knowledge and hands-on skills.

**100% READY
TO ENTER THE
CYBER WORKFORCE**

Figure 7.2 Cyversity red team training program, made possible by Google

The Power of Diversity and Inclusion in Cybersecurity

Joshua had a vision and a request: if he could assemble like-minded people who wanted to learn about red teaming, would I and Security Innovation be willing to help? Of course, the answer was yes, so I challenged Joshua to go sign up some folks and told him we'd talk again in a couple of weeks. Before 10 days had passed, Joshua had 50 people signed on!

After talking with my team at Security Innovation, we decided to duplicate the red team training program in its entirety for all 50 people. We planned it for the summer of 2022 and flew our lead instructor, Kevin Poniatowski, to Accra for a full day of on-site instructor-led training using our Application Security cyber range. Naturally, Joshua was thrilled. A few weeks after we ran the on-site event in Accra, he was off to Cincinnati. We ran the same training program again in the summer of 2023, this time with Joshua observing from San Diego, as he was in the midst of his internship at Intuit.

About that internship at Intuit ... Joshua was inspired by his success in reaching out to me in early 2022. He was encouraged to continue to reach out to others, network, and stretch his comfort zone so that his natural shyness wouldn't be an impediment to his career. I helped him craft abstracts and apply for speaking opportunities at conferences. He has now spoken at a few and is on a new mission: to speak one day at an RSA Conference. At one of those conferences, he met another amazing man, Kim Jones. Kim has had an illustrious career in cybersecurity, but at the time he and Joshua met, Kim was working at Intuit. Kim implored Joshua to apply for one of that company's cyber internships; thus, Joshua went on a sojourn to Southern California and the Pacific Ocean.

If nothing else, this case study illustrates the power of putting together several key pieces to build an effective initiative that can be transformative to the lives of underrepresented demographics like Joshua. One of his LinkedIn posts after he completed the scholarship program is self-evident.

"Cyversity, Security Innovation, Ed Adams, and Google made their mark giving me a life-changing skill that I am currently using in practice. Will recommend everyone check out Cyversity and Security Innovation for the awesome services and scholarships they have in store."

— *Joshua Offe Berkoh*

Closing Thoughts on Building D&I Programs

Underrepresentation in the cybersecurity industry is a multifaceted issue that demands urgent attention. Gender disparity, racial and ethnic underrepresentation, and intersectionality all contribute to the lack of diversity in the industry. By acknowledging and addressing these disparities, we can create a more inclusive and resilient cybersecurity workforce that better serves the needs of a rapidly evolving digital landscape. The time has come for collective action to bridge the gaps, empower underrepresented groups, and ensure that the cybersecurity industry reflects the diversity of our society.

There are many helpful guides that talk about how to build, roll out, and measure a D&I program, so I won't go into exhaustive details. However, here are a few things that I've personally experienced and heard from others to keep in mind:

- If you form a D&I committee, make sure the committee itself is diverse. Rotate membership to ensure new folks are included continuously for fresh perspectives.

- Set goals. Where are you today? Where do you want to be? How will you assess progress? How do you compare with industry averages? Do you even care about industry averages?

- Manage your goals:

  - Who is the primary champion/committee/facilitator?

  - Get equal collaboration between groups.

- Group goals into immediate, short-term, and long-term objectives.

- Revisit goals and priorities based on progress, market dynamics, changes at your organization, and so on. Goals will be fluid.

- Be realistic—things won't change overnight. We have a massive supply problem for new diverse cyber talent; changing that takes time and commitment.

- One-time consensus building and five-year plans don't work. Be realistic—start with some winnable goals that everyone agrees with and build from there.

- Take a very close look at your HR policies, hiring practices, and job descriptions with a critical eye to hiring/recruiting biases, word sensitivity, and qualifications.

Don't spend months writing your plan. You can refine it in time. The strategy will evolve, and things will change. The most important step is the declaration of the initiatives and hitting some wins quickly. The first steps is to get yourself in the game.

Summary

This chapter addressed the vital role of diversity and inclusion in cybersecurity, emphasizing its importance in combating a wide range of cyber threats. The chapter began by referencing a study by the Ponemon Institute, which surveyed cybersecurity practitioners in the United States about the state of diversity in their organizations. The findings point toward the current shortfall in achieving a diverse talent pool in cybersecurity.

The chapter defined diversity in cybersecurity as the representation of individuals from varied demographics, including race, gender, age, sexual orientation, disability, education, work experience, and cultural background. Inclusion, on the other hand, is about creating an environment where these diverse individuals feel valued and empowered to contribute. The chapter highlighted the critical need for D&I in building effective cybersecurity defenses, as diverse teams with varied skill sets and backgrounds can better understand and anticipate attackers' tactics.

The benefits of D&I in cybersecurity are manifold, including enhanced problem-solving, improved decision-making, heightened innovation, and creativity. The chapter cited research from reputable firms like Harvard Business Review, McKinsey, Catalyst, and Deloitte, all support the notion that diverse teams outperform homogeneous ones in various aspects.

However, the cybersecurity industry currently faces challenges like a shortage of skilled talent and a lack of diversity. The chapter discussed the underrepresentation of women and racial and ethnic minorities in the field. It highlighted the concept of intersectionality, recognizing that individuals with multiple marginalized identities face compounded discrimination. Addressing these disparities is crucial to building a more robust cybersecurity workforce.

To combat underrepresentation, the chapter suggests several approaches, including promoting cybersecurity education among underrepresented groups, government initiatives and policies for supporting diverse students, and industry collaboration. It also emphasized the need for realistic job descriptions and entry-level positions that truly require no previous professional experience.

The chapter concluded by stressing the importance of D&I in cybersecurity, not just as a business imperative but as a social and economic necessity. I provided several case studies of professionals, students, and executives to illustrate how various people develop themselves and others through D&I programs.

Embracing diversity and inclusion is fundamental to building robust defense mechanisms, fostering innovation, and improving decision-making in the cybersecurity industry. The collective effort is required to bridge the gaps, empower underrepresented groups, and ensure that the cybersecurity workforce reflects the diversity of society.

Chapter 8

Straight from the Heart (of Cyber)

"There are so many different facets and faces to cybersecurity! And many of the cyber roles don't require programming. In fact, some of my best team members have been history majors, psych majors, criminal justice. . . . A little curiosity is really all it takes!"

—Marnie Wilking, CISO and cyber executive at Booking .com, Wayfair, Wells Fargo, and others

This chapter was both the most difficult and enjoyable to write. It was enjoyable because I got to revisit the many conversations I had and survey results with people who were a major source of input and research for this book. It was difficult because I had to distill tens of thousands of words and data points into a short, cohesive summary—capturing what is nearly 200 collective years of cybersecurity experience among the many people who contributed input. But this is where we see the color wheel in action, sometimes in motion, as people migrate from slice to slice. This information, "straight from the heart" as I named it, is illuminating and illustrative. It provides a lot of context and real-world experiences that are tough to research without a lot of personal conversations.

I organize this chapter into two major sections.

- **Summary of key findings:** Here I distill the data provided in both surveys divided into topics that I hope you find useful.

- Getting into the cybersecurity industry

- Advice from practitioners

- Overcoming common challenges

- What hiring managers look for

- **Case studies:** This was a very challenging section, indeed, as there were many stories and examples that I had to leave "on the cutting room floor," so to speak. I chose several case studies that represent what I feel are an interesting representation of cyber journeys across various career paths.

As I wrote and rewrote this chapter, I was often reminded of this quote from Oprah Winfrey: "Know what sparks the light in you so that you, in your own way, can illuminate the world." This theme resonated over and over with the 150 people I interviewed. Before I dive into research results, I want to review a couple of key themes covered in this book.

As discussed in various chapters, there are many different types of security jobs, reflecting colors that show how offensive versus defensive each is, as well as the percentage of security responsibilities that comprise it. Colors aside, there are four "types" of jobs with varying degrees of deep technical, security, and business skills. At a higher and more conceptual level, here's how I see the cybersecurity color wheel as a gradient or continuum—from security as a core function to security as a job enabler.

- **Security as a core function:** Typically this is part of the infosec, SOC, or cybersecurity teams. Often (though not always) a technical background is useful or necessary here.

- **Technical functions:** These are IT staff, developers, program managers, DevOps, and others responsible for technology development and maintenance, where security skills move from nice-to-haves to must-haves.

- **Business as a core function/skill with a focus on the security business:** This focuses on security as a business, financial, and legal risks. The core of these jobs is something other than security—for example, governance, risk, compliance, and audit—but security drives a lot of their activities. Importantly, most of these jobs do not have technical baselines, degrees, or core requirements.

- **Security as a job enabler:** Even further afield from the previous category, these are folks in marketing, sales, product management, customer support, and other market-focused jobs where security knowledge builds credibility with prospects and shapes product development.

Another way to look at this is the simplified chart in Figure 8.1, plotting some common job functions on two axes: security-specific and technical. I used some work roles from the three primary π, and at the risk of sounding like a cliché, there is no typical path to security-related jobs.

It's also important to debunk the typical myths and stereotypes of security folks or security jobs. A decade ago, most CISOs were former engineers, were hackers, or had roots in other security functions. While they could have great conversations with technical and security teams, as security became more of a business and risk function, their ability to lead became limited; they had to evolve or be passed by business-thinking infosec professionals. This is not to say deep technical and security skills aren't important for some roles—for some, such as red teamers, they are critical. However, today it is important to think about what the position seeks to accomplish *first* and work backward from there—what skills are needed? Risk? Business? Legal? Communication? Writing? Many of the same skills we look for when hiring a CEO, marketer, product manager, and so on, are also critical for security positions. As you'll see from one of the core research questions covered later in this chapter, these "soft skills" are increasingly valued by hiring managers in cybersecurity.

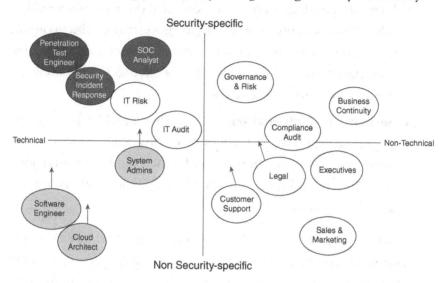

Figure 8.1 Cybersecurity jobs as a function of technical expertise

My journey to security was atypical as well; however, I'm realizing now that is how many cybersecurity careers started (atypically). I was an English and engineering double-major as an undergraduate at university. Immediately after graduating, I worked in engineering firms building nonlethal weapons systems. I realized I was drawn to computing technology and particularly to the software I was using to perform my engineering work. I also noticed that many of my fellow engineers would ask me to help them prepare and/or present their work, as they struggled with the communications elements of their job. At the time, I didn't realize just how valuable these writing and communication skills would be to my career; they have, in fact, been invaluable. Knowing I wanted to get more into the business of IT and software, I conducted a self-assessment. I found I was lacking in some fundamental business skills—corporate finance, marketing, business analytics, operations and supply chain, and so on.

That put me on a path to get a master's degree in business administration (MBA) and then focus on the software industry. After a decade of focusing on software functionality, resilience, performance, and so on, the next natural step was the other aspect of software quality that was forgotten or ignored at the time—security. Over the years, my literature learning background helped with my speaking skills and enabled me to write this book, deliver talks to thousands, and be a strong communicator.

I was fortunate to find a like-minded person in Dr. James A. Whittaker, who at the time was a professor at Florida Tech. He was ready to start a software security company with a group of his graduate and PhD students. I had paved my path, and our partnership was born. This is why there is no such thing as a typical starting point for security—many different skills are needed to be successful. Keep this in mind if you're pursuing a career in cybersecurity, but also if you're looking to hire, develop, and retain talent in your own organization. Great talent comes from varying places, and many could be hiding right under your nose, so to speak.

Regardless of the path you choose, you must continually learn and stay up-to-date on the latest cybersecurity trends and threats—this is crucial to your ongoing success. The security field is dynamic; threats, attacks, and technologies change rapidly. While not every job requires deep security expertise, every job requires staying abreast regularly. This is why it's a field of passion for most—it's an industry that naturally intrigues us. Learning is not a chore; it is a choice we willingly make.

My final comment before diving into some of the research findings is that building relationships in the cybersecurity community is another necessary activity. It is virtually impossible to succeed alone. This is true in most areas of life, but it is especially true in cybersecurity. It is a team sport, best played with diverse teammates. Following your passion, finding your light, and pursuing relevant training and certifications can open doors to positions in the field you might never have thought possible.

Survey and Insights: Word on the Streets

There are many paths to cyber jobs, as described in the previous chapters. To provide context, I reached out to about 150 of my peers in the space for their thoughts, tips, what got them interested in the space, and so on. Their experience levels ranged from entry level to 20+ years, with varying seniority and numerous titles such as product managers, learning and development, student, CISO, CEO, and more. I inquired about how they got started in security, the challenges they had to overcome, essential traits they seek beyond the résumé, and advice for those looking to get into or master the security industry.

The goal was to identify some trends as well as get some open-ended, real-world insight based on direct feedback. Note that this was an informal questionnaire; no methodology was vetted nor should it be used as empirical data to draw industry-wide conclusions. This was a learning experience for me as well, given the surprising amount of "other" selections chosen as answers. This once again reconfirms the fact that there are many different paths and instigators into security-related jobs.

Summary of Key Findings

This is a summary of my key findings:

- **Mentors** are critical; more than 80 percent had a mentor or inspirational leader prior to or during their cybersecurity journey.
- **Networking** is just as powerful as a strong résumé. Meeting others in the field, being introduced to new leaders and

companies, and getting involved in the cybersecurity community lead to very positive outcomes. Often, networking is even more important than holding a degree or industry certification because it can open doors unique to you and the networking path you take.

- Keep an **open mind**. Many people got into cybersecurity "by accident," never intending to do so at all. Others cite that they got lucky and an opportunity presented itself. Personally, I believe that we make a lot of our own luck (see the previous two bullets for "luck inspiration"), and more than one-third of respondents ended up in security via some tangential technical or business jobs, often the result of an internal corporate initiative for which they took responsibility (and initiative).

This data supports the notion that security requires mentoring and knowledge building. That takes folks by surprise when being introduced to it and serves as a reminder that success in cybersecurity is a team effort, whether you're building a career or managing a security program.

Getting Into Cybersecurity

Of the 146 people I asked "How did you first get the cybersecurity industry, i.e., get your first job?" 142 responded. I was surprised to learn that only about 25 percent pursued a cyber job directly or through a related association (nonprofit, school, and so on). Nearly 75 percent got into cybersecurity by accident or via some early/mid-career self-realization (see Figure 8.2). Some of these seeming anomalies can be explained by the fact that cybersecurity careers, as such, were far rarer in the early to mid 2000s (the point at which about a third of respondents entered the field).

Straight from the Heart (of Cyber)

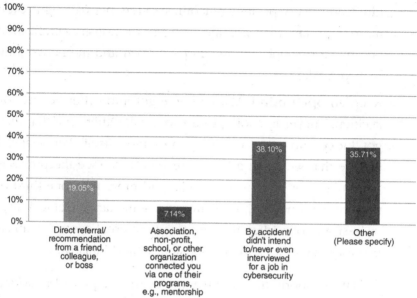

How did you **first enter** the cybersecurity industry, i.e., get your first job? (choose only ONE answer)
Answered: 142 Skipped: 4

Figure 8.2 Answers to the question "How did you first enter the cybersecurity industry?"

I found it fascinating that only 25 percent of the people surveyed got their first job via a direct referral or through a nonprofit or other association (including schools). Since so many people landed their first cybersecurity job either unintentionally or through some unorthodox, "other" means, I also asked each survey participant what first got them interested in the cybersecurity field. There, I also found no strong correlation to the three sparks I anticipated being cited: school, family/friend, and news of a hack. Figure 8.3 shows the results.

This drove me to dig deeper into the research and have dozens of live conversations to uncover some common traits. I was able to refactor everyone's initial interest in cybersecurity (which was often concurrent with their first job but not always) into three major categories.

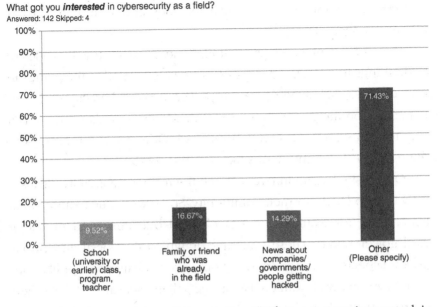

What got you *interested* in cybersecurity as a field?
Answered: 142 Skipped: 4

Figure 8.3 Answers to the question "What got you interested in cybersecurity as a field?"

- Compelled to it ("It's how I am wired")
- Career/on-the-job encouragement from others
- Self-realization during a nonsecurity career

Compelled: "It's How I Am Wired"

Personality-wise, people who are drawn to security often have a natural tendency to tinker. They want to understand how things function and fail and what is going on behind the scenes. Many are prolific tinkerers are curious by nature and exhibit these traits at a young age, being drawn to challenges, especially hands-on "beat/cheat the systems" challenges. They tend to fall into security naturally, as it aligns with their personality. This is an inherent personality trait that is invaluable in cybersecurity, where things are always changing and constant improvement (which includes understanding what is broken) is needed.

Many of my interviewees exhibited these traits, citing their desire to do things like crack video games—be able to modify the games in various ways such as improve the power of your character—or coding games on the graphic calculators handed out in high school as a way to deal with the boredom of school. Others found their way to things like *Phrack* and books like *The Puzzle Palace*.

Others still had an inherent "catch the robbers" mentality altruistically to help clients or their community. Some were due to a personal experience, for example, "I was phished one time, and my debit card got emptied." These folks are drawn to the social and public policy aspects of cybersecurity. Some were designing applications or IT systems and wanted to protect client sensitive data; others oversaw technology solutions (as a product manager, for example) and wanted to ensure customers didn't pay for or inherit the security mistakes the development teams were so obviously making.

Several in this category were hooked after "dipping their toe" into the security waters, which supports the field's dynamic nature that attracts a wide range of people. There are few I've met that say they tried security and didn't like it—and those who didn't have a fully positive experience were often still hooked and inspired to find the "right" area of cybersecurity for them (which would ultimately be different than the one they first tried). This is why cybersecurity is so often a career of passion. People who feel compelled to be in the security industry, somehow, some way, often serve as champions for their organization (not often by design). When the organization they're working for doesn't match their passion or commitment, the tenure there is usually short term.

Here are two relevant quotes from my conversations with people who are wired for security:

- "My purpose has always been to keep people safe. Once I left the military, this was the only career that truly made sense to me."

—CISO for tech and financial firms; now lecturer, trainer, and mentor. *Note the path from veteran to CISO.*

- "My origins in the industry are rooted in internal/external investigations for prosecution against fraud, theft, and embezzlement. I truly enjoyed facing intelligent and crafty threats and working to predict, prevent, detect, and respond to their malicious actions!"

—Cybersecurity strategist, author, and keynote speaker who first was nudged into cybersecurity by his boss. *Note the initial interest in fraud and financial embezzlement!*

Career/On-the-Job Encouragement from Others

Today, a career in cybersecurity is a legitimate path one might consider as early as a teenager. After all, cybersecurity news is everywhere and information technology dominates our lives. But frequently, cybersecurity is recommended to someone who gets involved, sometimes unwillingly, and later learns to love the industry and make a career of it. This theme cropped up frequently in my research. Many indicated that they got into security after finding out about a new regulation or legislation that impacted their job. Others cited client demands, new partnerships, or their company's response to a breach involving their product or area of focus at work. These newly inherited responsibilities and newly realized internal organizational needs lit a spark that most didn't know existed. The initial foray into cybersecurity for many of these folks was viewed as a necessity of their job. They had been selected by their employer to lead up a special program and/or introduce security to their team(s) who previously had been blissfully security agnostic.

For individuals considering whether the cybersecurity industry is right for you, the takeaway from these interview responses is to keep an open mind. Take that first step and explore. Maybe you won't like it at all; maybe you will. Either way, you will have learned something about cybersecurity and, I predict, it won't be the last thing you learn about it. For managers and recruiters looking for cybersecurity talent in their own workforce, the message is to creatively inquire. People who can step up to cyber are everywhere. Do not assume they need a technical background to be a significant contributor to the cybersecurity hygiene of your company; it is not true. Everyone starts somewhere, so look for people who want to collaborate. Remember, the cybersecurity color wheel is all about collaboration; it's the only way to break out of the primary colors. So, always be on the lookout for opportunities to shift security *into* other groups as well as recruiting security professionals from other groups in your organization. It works well in both directions. Be sensitive, but don't be afraid to poke your nose into other initiatives. You may find a diamond in the rough...better yet, you may find a handful!

I provide some examples of people who inherited a security job function or responsibility through the encouragement of others. As with the previous examples, pay attention to the job they were currently in as well as the impetus for the transition into cybersecurity. You may find something familiar in the short stories. Ideally, it inspires you to dive into the field or encourage others to do so, even if it's part of the same job. Remember, adding security skills to your current repertoire, in and of itself, is a valuable thing.

"As an investment banker, no sector has broader appeal (every one needs cyber DNA) or a greater range of emerging potential clients!" is a telling quote that came from someone I respect quite a lot. She's a woman who created a niche as a broker of cybersecurity companies. She helps other companies and investors buy and sell cybersecurity firms. Does it sound like fun being the catalyst for flipping cyber firms? If you don't know what an investment banker does, think of them like a real estate agent. They are responsible for pairing up buyers and sellers of a particular asset, in this case, cybersecurity companies as opposed to a house. What is this amazing woman's background and education you may ask yourself? She has an economic undergraduate degree and an MBA. She started her career as a financial analyst where she researched (read: learned) about companies in the broad high-tech space, including companies that focused on data protection.

She developed an interest in cybersecurity as part of this job and decided to explore it more, first as part of her job and later by taking the bold step to start her own investment banking company with a partner and specialize in the cybersecurity industry. At the time, her company was one of the very few doing this type of exclusive investment banking. Today, they have offices in the United States, United Kingdom, and Israel and are the go-to resource for cybersecurity entrepreneurs looking to sell their companies.

Here is another interesting thing I heard:

> "I was definitely not looking for a cybersecurity job. I was looking for an internship in computer networks and my former boss was looking for college students to continue his research in an open-source project. So, I ended up working on an open-source project called UCSniff, a VoIP vulnerability assessment tool, and improved it to include real-time eavesdropping."

From that point, this young man was hooked. Another person I interviewed also found security via a nonsecurity internship: "I had an internship during a time when a corporate security initiative was being launched. Nobody else on my intern team wanted to head it up, so they gave it to me. After that, I continued to love security."

Straight from the Heart (of Cyber)

Others had more cybersecurity wheel color-specific origin stories. One person was working on his IT job—a regular "keep the employees happy" type of endpoint management work role. Then his employer experienced its first online breach. Even though others were primarily responsible, he asked questions as a curious young professional (and good for him, by the way!). The response? "Why don't you look into it?" From that point forward, he was responsible for finding the source of the breach. He wasn't particularly interested in cybersecurity; but, he was given a task by his boss and did his job. The result was a career. Consider those last five words once more, if you please. *The result was a career.* You never know where you'll end up, but it always starts with a first step in some direction.

These examples notwithstanding, many cybersecurity professionals do start their careers as technical professionals. Many, like me, get engineering degrees and then morph into some type of quality role. There's one individual in my survey who was a software engineer; however, in his own words, "I consistently ran across security as a component to writing quality software as a software engineer." This sentiment is near and dear to my heart. In 2004, I created a slide for a software test automation company that expressed "an interest in security." That slide, which is still 100 percent valid today, was a pyramid. The pyramid showed security as aspects of software quality—like functionality, performance, reliability, and so on. At the time very few were thinking of security as part of the quality family, but, as a mechanical engineer, I was taught to calculate a "factor of safety" into every one of my designs. Safety (the point at which a physical system fails) is analogous to security in software. So I, too, was encouraged to join the security ranks when a colleague of mine decided to start a company built on the premise of software security.

One person I interviewed made a very simple, but transitionally telling, statement: "I was doing an internship coding and hated it.

They ask me to break code, and I loved it." This person, my friend Larry Whiteside Jr., went on to be a CISO and is an active mentor for others interested in cybersecurity careers. Another was referred into security by a co-worker: "A friend/colleague strongly recommended I join his AppSec team as an AppSec architect after seeing my contributions as an application/enterprise architect." Similarly, a pervasive industry regulation creates on-the-job opportunities. One interviewee in the oil and gas industry never considered security a career path; however, when "Payment Card Operations for Petroleum Retailers evolved into PCI-DSS…it catapulted the need to learn more about cybersecurity."

These examples reinforce the value of getting involved, both as an individual contributor and as a leader. Also, they emphasize how managers and co-workers often seek people with a certain passion or talent, cajoling them to give security a try. That creative thinking and initiative can transform a person's life as well as the organization for which they work.

Individually Pursued

Though similar to the previous section, that is, situations where someone else asked or encouraged someone to get into security (client, boss, and so on), this section is about people who proactively got into security on their own—sometimes by accident and sometimes by curiosity. These folks didn't have an innate passion for security, like the "compelled" folks, but they did discover the field on their own after they had started down some other career path.

One person I interviewed made an accidental discovery while writing code—a security vulnerability that allowed external code to execute in the application he was writing. This got him interested in security, but there was no such job at his current employer. So, he started looking for a job that had software security as a focus. In his own words,

Straight from the Heart (of Cyber)

"I got really, really lucky. A small application consultancy with strong academic leadership was taking a different approach to hiring security testers. Instead of requiring security experience, they looked for developers who understood how systems were built, and therefore may be able to understand how those systems could also be destroyed. My background in development combined with their forward thinking provided the tiny opportunity I needed to explore a security career."

In that conversation, this person added a piece of advice, summarized as never forget that success in security is almost always a combination of your knowledge, mutual hard work, and someone else presenting you with an opportunity. Security careers are rarely made alone.

You might discover your job could stand for some security forethought. One person, who was working for a large printer manufacturer, was chartered with gathering competitive intelligence as part of her product management job. She discovered that some competing products were easily tampered with, resulting in lower overall quality, higher total cost of ownership, and poor customer satisfaction. She started including security requirements in her product specifications and go-to-market positioning. From there, other product teams started doing the same. Eventually, the organization formed an "Office of Product Security," and she got a lead position with the firm. This anti-tamper angle into security also worked for a colleague of mine who works for a microprocessor/computer chip manufacturer. Tampering with devices can impact the *confidentiality* of the data it's processing, the *integrity* of its function, and/or its *availability*. These are the three core tenants of security.

Some people in my research got into security because they were working on (or interested in) a security product their company was building and selling. One woman was in product management, similar to the woman described previously at the printer company. The flagship product of this firm, however, was a database. In her words, she first entered the cybersecurity industry when she "moved to a product management job in security-related features/functions of a product. I'd been eyeing that group for some time, and when there was an opening, I jumped on it." Opportunity presented itself, and she was bold enough to go for it. There's a reason the saying "fortune favors the bold" exists; she embodies that spirit.

Another man was in software development but working on a security product. The product got him hooked, and that interest helped him launch a career spent as an application security lead at large organizations. His primary job has been to build security standards for software development teams, train those teams on security, and serve as a go-to subject-matter expert when any of the teams need help. Similarly, another man I interviewed was working for a bank that had suffered an "electronic crime event," which is another way of saying the bank got hacked. He observed, "The need of the hour was to create a framework to document and tackle technology-related crime in the financial services sector. My involvement there shaped my career thereafter." He went on to serve as co-head of application security at one of the largest IT services firms on the planet.

I heard several examples of people who applied for a job in compliance (a white team job on the cybersecurity color wheel) that happened to be in the information security department. Exposure to red and blue team jobs sparked an interest in a direct career in cybersecurity. Finally, one person who has no college degree caught the cybersecurity bug while selling IT services. This is a job that's "off" the color wheel. I share more examples like this later in this chapter; however, this person learned about patch management and associated vulnerabilities as he was selling non-security-related IT services. He saw the need and growing interest in IT security and decided to

Straight from the Heart (of Cyber)

seek a job selling IT security products and services. Eventually, he decided to start his own company doing that very thing. Today, he is a successful, well-known entrepreneur and also serves as a mentor to others.

Unsure Where to Start?

For those unsure of what they want to do, a few recommendations for you include volunteering, doing an internship (paid or free), and/or joining an organization at an entry-level position that requires little security experience but provides the opportunity to learn from others. Any one of these can help you figure out where your passions lie in cybersecurity and which industry certifications might help you develop your skills, if at all. Remember, security opportunities can be found in almost any organization.

The next sections include a few thoughts for those looking to build skills to land their first job.

Internships

Internships are great for potential security prospects and employers alike—allowing an opportunity to identify those with a passion for security and to "try before you buy." If can't get a paid internship, consider volunteering to be an intern. Ask if an organization you like or know would give you an internship for a few months. Be proactive. Many firms have a formal (and usually paid) internship program, but getting direct experience is the most important thing. LinkedIn, Glassdoor, Simply Hired, Monster.com, Dice, and other sites list such internships, and you can even filter on skills and ability. Starting a career in security can begin with internships and entry-level positions that help you gain experience and build foundational knowledge. Some organizations offer trainee positions in various security domains, providing valuable hands-on experience and mentorship.

If you aren't part of a cybersecurity nonprofit or association, consider joining. Some are targeted at particular demographics; others are open to all. These groups often have very valuable programs like mentorship, job boards, free training, connections to internship programs, and industry certifications that can help launch your career.

Entry-Level Positions

There's a dirty little secret in the cybersecurity world that some of us are trying to rub out. The Catch-22 is that many "entry-level" jobs still want one or two years of experience. If possible, find a way to do something cybersecurity related in your current job—help out in the SOC or offer to aid an investigation into a security incident. Look for opportunities for hands-on experience that's related in any way, and be sure to add this to your résumé. Many companies will consider equivalencies like this in lieu of the hard requirement. When in doubt, ask. You may be surprised how many hiring managers view some of the requirements in a job description as "nice to have" despite listing them as necessary qualifications. One hiring manager I interviewed said, "We need more diverse skills in cybersecurity. In my opinion, for an entry-level person, traits like the desire to learn, curiosity, and teamwork are *more* important than resume skills, education, and knowledge." Be bold. Be encouraged. Don't be afraid of rejection.

In reality, many entry-level work roles do not require security skills. These are jobs like analysts, specialists, associates, and positions that entail reactive responsibilities such as monitoring, documenting, classifying assets, writing impact assessments, writing policies, and other tasks that will introduce you to technology and security concepts. There are many jobs in which you learn as you go. For example, an identity and access management (IAM) technician could be responsible for using a checklist to compare configurations

Straight from the Heart (of Cyber)

and ensure the IAM controls were set up properly. A junior penetration test engineer could be using a specific tool only to run scans on a web app. Often the tools themselves have learning assets, so when they find a vulnerability like SQL injection or cross-site scripting, they provide information about those flaws, which will help you learn about them as you operate and learn about the scanning product.

Here is a relatively accessible red team job to consider when starting a cybersecurity career. This tends to have a more technical bent to it; however, after this example, I list some positions that are more business focused.

Junior Pentester/Vulnerability Specialist

Positions like vulnerability analyst/assessor, junior pentester, and so on, allow you to learn about hacking and vulnerability assessment while assisting with very prescriptive tasks. A vulnerability assessment specialist is responsible for identifying, analyzing, and mitigating vulnerabilities in an organization's information systems, networks, and infrastructure. Their primary goal is to proactively assess and address security weaknesses to prevent potential security breaches, data leaks, and other cyber threats.

Here's a breakdown of what a vulnerability assessment specialist typically does:

- **Risk assessment:** Assesses the risks associated with vulnerabilities, taking into account the organization's specific context and potential impacts on data, operations, and compliance.

- **Reporting:** Generates comprehensive reports detailing the vulnerabilities discovered, including their potential impact and recommended remediation steps. These reports are typically shared with IT teams, management, and stakeholders.

See Yourself in Cyber

- **Remediation planning:** Collaborates with IT and security teams to develop plans for addressing and mitigating vulnerabilities. This may involve recommending software patches, configuration changes, or security measures.

- **Vulnerability scanning:** Conducts regular scans of an organization's IT systems and networks using automated vulnerability scanning tools. These scans identify known vulnerabilities in software, hardware, and configurations.

- **Manual testing:** In addition to automated scans, performs manual testing to identify vulnerabilities that automated tools might miss. This could involve a more in-depth analysis of specific systems or applications.

- **Vulnerability assessment:** Evaluates the severity and potential impact of identified vulnerabilities and prioritizes vulnerabilities based on their risk and potential for exploitation.

- **Testing remediation:** Verifies that the vulnerabilities have been effectively remediated by retesting the systems and confirming that the vulnerabilities are no longer present.

- **Compliance and regulatory alignment:** Ensures that the organization's vulnerability management processes align with industry standards, best practices, and any regulatory requirements applicable to the organization.

- **Security awareness and training:** Helps educate and train employees and IT staff about security best practices and how to report vulnerabilities or security concerns.

- **Incident response support:** Assists in security incident response efforts by identifying vulnerabilities that may have been exploited during an incident and helps to determine the scope of an attack.

- **Research and updates:** Stays current with emerging threats and vulnerabilities by researching new security issues and keeping up-to-date with software and system updates.

- **Security policies:** Contributes to the development and maintenance of security policies, procedures, and guidelines for vulnerability management within the organization.

> To increase your chances of landing a technical entry-level security job, consider obtaining relevant certifications, such as CompTIA Security+, Certificate of Cloud Security Knowledge (CCSK), Certified in Cyber (CC), or Certified Ethical Hacker (CEH.) ISACA offers short and fairly inexpensive certificates for cybersecurity, cloud auditing, and popular technologies businesses run on that need to be secured, such as IoT, blockchain, and artificial intelligence.

For those more interested in a business-centric cybersecurity career, you can find entry-level risk analysts, auditor, or other specialists who typically work under the supervision of more experienced professionals. Over time, these roles may take on more complex tasks and responsibilities as you gain experience and expertise in risk management. The specific duties and focus of each role can vary widely between industries, including finance, insurance, healthcare, and others, but the fundamental goal is to help the organization understand, assess, and mitigate risks to achieve its objectives while safeguarding its assets and reputation.

- **Privacy/compliance associate/specialist:** This specialist helps ensure organizations are in compliance. This is a good starting point for those interested in the regulatory side of cybersecurity, performing tasks such as reading new regulations, documenting changes, and updating policies and disseminating them to other groups. It typically includes identifying areas of noncompliance (training, policies, release cycles, data privacy, and so on) as well as documenting breaches and events, recordkeeping, documenting third-party compliance, and assembling reports for audits.

- **Risk analyst (entry level):** Entry-level positions may focus on data-risk analysis and basic risk management tasks. Tasks include data crunching and analysis, preparing reports, maintaining documentation, research and information gathering, assisting in the assessment of financial, operational, compliance, strategic, and other types of risks. This includes identifying potential risk factors and evaluating their potential impact on the organization. They use risk management software and tools to facilitate data analysis and reporting.

- **Security awareness trainer:** Security awareness trainers educate employees about security best practices. This role focuses on building a security-conscious culture in the organization.

- **Privacy and data analyst:** These officers focus on ensuring that an organization complies with data privacy laws and protects sensitive information.

- **Security program associate:** This role includes reporting and metrics, policy updating, and supporting technical professionals across a wide range of cybersecurity initiatives.

ISACA is a leader in GRC learning and certification, offering both comprehensive and shorter programs in information systems, cybersecurity, audit, data privacy, and governance. It's essential to choose a GRC certification that aligns with your career goals and the specific industry in which you work. These certifications often require a combination of work experience, passing an exam, and continuing education to maintain the certification. Additionally, the value of certification can vary depending on the job market and employer requirements, so it's a good idea to research the demand for specific certifications in your field and region. Also, consider a Certified Information Systems Security Professional (CISSP) or Certified Cloud Security Professional (CCSP) after you have a few years of experience. While not GRC-specific, many GRC roles require strong information security knowledge, and these are still the gold standard of cybersecurity industry certifications.

Broad vs. Specialized Skills

In the field of cybersecurity, there are various specialties and job roles to ensure effective security practices and protection of digital assets. These roles all involve varying degrees of interaction with people, processes, and technology to create a comprehensive security strategy and protect an organization's assets from cybersecurity threats.

For those who know what they want to do, it's often favorable to pick a specialization and become a master at it. For those unsure, going broad might be beneficial. However, fundamental (and battle-tested) security principles are always a no-brainer. Technologies, attacks, and threats change daily. However, essential security principles (for example, defense-in-depth, zero trust) and attack techniques are time-tested and provide the high-level mentality that everyone in the security profession needs.

Once you have a solid grasp of the basic fundamental security skills, consider getting into a specific technology, standard, or framework more deeply. The foundational skills are applicable, whether you are trying to quantify risk, understand your attack surface, or build more resilient systems. Each discipline builds on those skills to get into technology, standard, and framework-specific disciplines.

This is part of the value of "getting security"—if you understand it at a high level, you can work your way toward almost anything.

In contrast to learning high-level fundamentals, another approach is to master at least one technical area very deeply. Remember that cybersecurity is a diverse field, and there are various specialties. Without getting into specific titles in this particular section, I encourage you to think more freely about the objective and impact of this type of job. It can be a two-edged sword, so to speak. Specialization can make you highly valued in an organization; however, it can also create a typecast with which you are associated—this can be difficult to break away from when and if you want to do so. I do not view it as a significant risk, but it is one of which to be aware. If you gravitate toward the technical areas of cybersecurity, you may be very well suited to learn as much as you can about a specific technology, such as the Google Cloud Platform, to help pave your way as a cloud security expert. You also may want to consider learning a specific technique or framework, such as MITRE ATT&CK, to help pave your way as an exploitation specialist or penetration tester. Unlike the business side of cybersecurity, which involves more reporting, analysis, working with people, reducing risk, and ensuring compliance, these specialization roles are hands-on technical and usually involve working with yellow teams to help ensure the safe deployment and operation of digital assets.

People vs. Process vs. Technology Focus

One more lens to consider as you're getting started in cybersecurity is whether you want to focus on the people aspect, the process aspect, or the technology aspect. While almost every job that deals with cybersecurity spans technology risk, process enablement, and elevating security awareness/skills, most tend to focus on one area primarily.

People

Virtually all security roles require some degree of interaction with people, but these positions emphasize direct engagement with employees, stakeholders, and teams to address security concerns, educate on best practices, or manage security programs that involve human factors. In many businesses, various positions involve security as part of their job responsibilities, even if security is not their primary focus. This is often referred to as *security awareness* or *security culture*. Such positions help promote and maintain a culture of security throughout the organization. The business positions in this section deal with security as part of their job.

These roles may not have security as their primary responsibility, but they are crucial for promoting and maintaining a strong security culture and ensuring that security practices are integrated into various aspects of the business. Building security awareness and best practices throughout an organization is essential in today's cybersecurity landscape.

- **Human resources (HR):** HR professionals are responsible for onboarding new employees, which includes educating them about security policies and practices. HR may also be involved in conducting background checks and ensuring that employees adhere to security guidelines.

- **Communications and public relations:** These departments can help manage the organization's response to security incidents, including managing public relations during data breaches and other security-related incidents.

- **Project management:** Project managers may integrate security requirements into project plans, ensuring that security considerations are addressed when implementing new systems or processes.

- **Executive leadership:** Company executives set the tone for security in an organization by supporting and advocating for security initiatives, even though security is not their primary responsibility.

- **Marketing:** Marketing teams can be responsible for communicating the organization's commitment to security to customers and stakeholders, demonstrating a commitment to protecting data and privacy.

- **Security awareness trainer:** Security awareness trainers are dedicated to educating and engaging people in the organization. Their primary focus is on raising security awareness, training employees on security best practices, and fostering a security-conscious culture. They interact directly with people to impart knowledge and build a human-centric security approach.

- **Recruiting/learning and development:** These professionals may create security training programs and materials for employees to ensure they are aware of and follow security policies and practices.

- **Cybersecurity education and training manager:** With the growing need for cybersecurity awareness, these managers develop and implement training programs and materials to educate employees about security best practices.

Process, Policies, and Governance/Legal

As security inherently moves from a technical to a business risk, the need for process and governance comes into focus. Cybersecurity has evolved from simply finding security holes and keeping malicious actors off the network to managing risk. For example, financial, legal, and reputation risk are all areas that security is quickly creeping into. Breaches cause financial and reputation losses, and organizations need to quantify this risk, which requires skills that go far beyond hacking, vulnerabilities, red teams, and defense.

Each of these roles involves integrating security considerations to protect the organization's assets, reputation, and compliance with relevant regulations. These professionals play a vital role in addressing the dynamic and ever-evolving field of cybersecurity.

Processes can range anywhere from secure software development practices to regulatory compliance to business policies. In the financial, legal, and risk management fields, security is an important and evolving subset that focuses on safeguarding assets, data, and information. Here are some positions in these areas that include security as a significant component:

- **Risk officer:** Risk officers in finance assess and manage various types of risks, including financial risks. They often consider cybersecurity risk and ensure that financial strategies include provisions for security-related expenses and contingencies.

- **Cybersecurity attorney:** These attorneys specialize in the legal aspects of cybersecurity, including regulatory compliance, data breach response, and intellectual property protection. They help organizations navigate the legal landscape of cybersecurity.

- **Privacy/compliance officer:** Privacy officers, often found in legal departments, focus on ensuring compliance with data protection laws and regulations. They play a key role in safeguarding customer data and information security.

- **Insurance risk manager:** These professionals work with insurance policies related to cybersecurity risks. They assess the financial impact of security.

- **Compliance and auditing:** While these roles have a primary focus on ensuring regulatory compliance, they often collaborate with various departments to assess security practices and identify areas of non-compliance. Compliance officers ensure that an organization adheres to relevant laws and regulations, including those related to data security and privacy. They work to develop, implement, and enforce security and compliance policies.

- **Privacy and data protection officer:** With the rise of data protection regulations like the GDPR and CCPA, these officers ensure that an organization complies with data privacy laws and protects sensitive information.

- **Chief financial officer (CFO)/financial analyst:** A CFO is responsible for the financial management of an organization, including overseeing financial security and risk management practices to protect assets, data, and financial transactions. They specialize in cybersecurity finance, focusing on evaluating investments in security technologies, calculating the financial impact of security breaches, and assessing the return on security investments.

- **Business continuity manager:** While primarily focused on disaster recovery and business continuity planning, these managers also address security aspects, ensuring the organization can recover from security incidents while minimizing financial losses.

- **Operational risk manager:** Operational risk managers consider a broad range of risks, including those related to information security and technology. They work to minimize disruptions and financial losses due to security incidents.

- **Ransomware recovery specialist:** Given the prevalence of ransomware attacks, these specialists focus on developing and implementing strategies for recovering from ransomware incidents.

- **Cybersecurity data analyst/scientist:** These professionals focus on analyzing and interpreting cybersecurity data to detect patterns, trends, and anomalies, helping organizations make informed security decisions.

- **Cybersecurity communications manager:** In this role, professionals focus on developing and managing internal and external cybersecurity communications, including incident response communications and security awareness campaigns.

Technology

Folks who work with technology are both directly and indirectly responsible for building security into design, integrating components security, operating and deploying in cloud safely, and so on. For example, a software engineer and security engineer have overlapping responsibilities, as I covered in Chapter 4. The following roles and titles primarily focus on technology aspects within the realm of cybersecurity:

- **Security engineering:** These people are heavily involved in designing, implementing, and maintaining an organization's security infrastructure, which includes configuring and managing various security technologies and tools. Their primary responsibility is to ensure that technology solutions effectively protect digital assets.

- **Software, network, security architects:** Security architects focus on designing the overall security strategy and infrastructure of an organization. Their primary role is to incorporate security into the design of software and systems to provide more resiliency and to integrate technology solutions that align with the security goals and business requirements.

- **Office of product security:** Jobs here range from junior level to chief product security officer (CPSO). This group is responsible for understanding customer needs regarding product security and data privacy and ensuring expectations are met. It identifies and ensures compliance with all relevant regulations and standards.

- **Vulnerability assessment and management:** This has been covered extensively in other sections; however, the focus is identifying and remediating security vulnerabilities in technology solutions and security flaws in technology systems.

- **Digital forensics:** Digital forensics analysts use technology to investigate security incidents, collect digital evidence, and perform forensic analyses on devices and systems. Their role heavily relies on specialized technology and tools. They work with technology and interact with law enforcement and legal teams as necessary.

- **Security operations center (SOC) analyst:** SOC analysts monitor security alerts, respond to incidents, and utilize various technology tools and solutions to manage and investigate security events.

- **Incident responder:** Incident responders are responsible for managing and mitigating security incidents. They work with people across the organization to coordinate responses, and they utilize technology to investigate and contain incidents.

Advice from Cybersecurity Practitioners

When the 150 people I interviewed were asked, "Which piece of advice would you give someone who is interested in entering the

199

cybersecurity industry?" nearly two-thirds of them recommended joining an association, nonprofit, or other organization where a newbie can learn and get connected with others. See Figure 8.4.

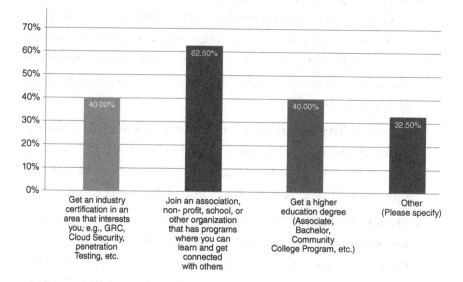

Figure 8.4 Answers to the question "Which piece of advice would you give someone who is interested in entering the cybersecurity industry?"

Forty percent recommended an industry certification, for example, GRC or Cloud Security, which was the same percentage who recommended obtaining some type of higher education degree, even from a community college or continuing education organization. Many of my interviewees had advice that went beyond the three standard answers I allowed them to select. I refactored all of their answers into these four categories:

- Find your passion.
- Try, learn, fail, repeat.

- Get involved.

- Network.

Find Your Passion and Have a Plan

So many people I interviewed stressed the importance of doing research in advance to find an area of cybersecurity that appeals to you. Several recommended checking out NIST's NICE cybersecurity framework (see `https://niccs.cisa.gov/workforce-development/nice-framework`) for technical positions and leveraging the free skills assessments available on the website. You can learn what skills are needed in the different cybersecurity jobs and how to contribute in either a technical or nontechnical role. Others suggested creating your own project—whether it's researching how to attack or defend a particular piece of technology or trying to build something on your own. Then, submit your work to a relevant industry conference where you can present/talk about it. You'll get smarter about something, and it's a great way to connect with different people.

Some people had quite specific recommendations; for example, find people on LinkedIn who have interesting jobs. Review their career path. Reach out to them and ask for advice. Multiple people suggested utilizing the numerous free and paid online education to build your skills. You may find that certain areas of cybersecurity you expected to like do not suit your fancy. Likewise, you may discover an unknown passion in a field previously unknown to you. Something like the Certified in Cybersecurity training and certification offered by (ISC2) is an example of a readily accessible training and certification program that provides a broad base of knowledge and learning. See `www.isc2.org/certifications/cc` for more information about this entry-level certification.

By far, the most common theme was to follow your passion and have a plan to get on a desired career track, which was offered from people ranging from CISOs to entry-level professionals who recently started their cybersecurity careers. Complementing the identification of passion, other advice included the need to develop good communication skills, problem-solving abilities, and teamwork, as cybersecurity often involves collaboration and explaining complex issues to nontechnical stakeholders. Learn how to think critically first so that when you do need to explain your work, you're able to answer the "why?" question, which is usually even more important than the "what?" or the "how?"

Learn and Get Practical/Hands-On Experience

While valuable, certificate programs and even four-year programs generally do not provide enough real-world, hands-on experience. It is crucial that you get practical experience. There are many free and paid resources to get hands-on practice and concept learning, both on and off the job. Many organizations are proactively seeking security talent and run programs that may interest you. These organizations also frequently offer some level of security training. Look to your organization's learning and development team or your human resources department; they may have free training available to you. Most will provide documentation and/or a certificate of participation and completion, which you can add to your résumé, work into interviews, and so on.

Here are some examples from the interviews I conducted:

- "Set up a test or lab environment to practice as you learn. This will allow you to gain real-world experience as you work toward gaining an industry certification." I can attest firsthand that this effort impresses hiring managers. I still recall my IT lead being torn between two candidates after interviews. Then one of them wrote to the hiring manager about how he had set up an Ubuntu Linux server on his own to learn it since that was the OS we were using for one of our key systems. That made the difference, and the proactive candidate got the job.

- "Participate in online capture-the-flag (CTFs) contests." These are a great way to get that war-gaming experience in a safe environment. I guarantee you'll leave the experience feeling a bit smarter than when you started.

- "Get free certifications—look to Cybrary, LinkedIn, and others."

- "Donate time on a security team, internal or external, just to learn." We often don't have time for this; however, if you already have a job, consider approaching the security team to ask them what or how you might be able to contribute to the security strategy or requirements at your organization.

- "Participate in bug bounty programs." For those who don't know what a bug bounty program is, many companies will offer money, prizes, or recognition if you find and report a security flaw in any of their products. Pay attention to the rules of engagement so you don't accidentally do anything that's viewed as a breach of trust or illegal hacking. Most companies document their bug bounty programs very thoroughly. Read the details.

CTFs test your cybersecurity knowledge and skills. They can be offered in a "Jeopardy-style" question/answer format, hands-on attack/defend, or mixed mode. They are offered for fun, learning, and often include prizes for top scores. They can be found attached to many cybersecurity conferences as well as stand-alone events.

One experienced cybersecurity professional cautioned, "Certificates often lack context for how to apply the knowledge unless you've been in the industry, so having access to updated (and hands-on) training content is critical." Ask your employer about what security training is offered to all employees and whether there are any hands-on labs or practice areas to hone the skills you learn in training.

Hiring managers and leaders should reinforce the need for their organization (and/or individual workers) to invest in commercial training. The vast majority of college degree programs, even technical ones such as computer science, still do not offer significant security education as part of those programs. Commercial vendors have an incentive to keep their content current and ensure it covers the latest and greatest technologies; otherwise, they'll lose the business to a competitor. Unlike four-year degrees and even certifications, which are, by design, not updated that often, an out-of-date commercial training catalog is quite uncommon.

There are countless articles that discuss a shortage of cybersecurity skills; cybersecurity skills shortage; yet, in many ways that shortage is the result of organizations having an expectation that they can easily hire a level 2 or 3 cybersecurity expert. Organizations are often reluctant to look at people who do not have specific certifications or credentials. I recommend that individuals interested in a cyber job do some research on what skill sets are valuable in cybersecurity. Look at the different types of work roles listed in cybersecurity workforce frameworks like NICE, paying particular attention to the tasks, knowledge, skills, and abilities they list as being necessary to succeed in each role. In the NICE Framework, these are known as TKSAs or KSAs.

Having a better understanding of what types of positions are available allows you to concentrate on getting the right certifications and training. It may lead to you pursuing a particular higher education degree and/or working with organizations that offer skills development programs. As referenced in several chapters in this book, there are numerous associations that offer free or steeply discounted educational and training resources. There is a wide range of material that is available on the Internet to steer people toward the best cybersecurity position for them.

The meta message of this section is that experience does matter. However, that experience can be self-created, earned as part of a certification program, and/or developed via volunteering your time (in addition to or as part of a current job). Earning a higher education degree is a great step toward advancing one's career; but, there are historical, cultural, social, and financial barriers to entry that make this challenging for certain demographics. This is where membership in associations and nonprofits geared at helping those demographics can be invaluable—transformative even.

Another sad truth about university degrees is that the curricula are often outdated before you graduate, so while they are good at teaching the basic fundamentals, many graduates must make an effort to stay up-to-date with current cybersecurity trends, attacks, technologies, and defense techniques. Be inquisitive. Security isn't just about hacking; find something you love doing, and there's probably a spot in security for you.

Get Involved/Create Visibility

Breaking into the cybersecurity industry and creating visibility involves a combination of identifying your passion, getting "smarter" about cyber by trying some different things, gaining any practical experience you can, networking (which I discuss after this section), and getting involved/creating visibility for yourself. This section has some suggestions to help inspire you to get more active in the cybersecurity industry.

Some of the folks I interviewed mentioned the value of creating personal projects and/or participating in cybersecurity competitions and hackathons. Those are great for experimentation and learning; however, to leverage them for career development, also consider promoting those projects in various online communities. To elevate your personal brand, consider joining professional cybersecurity groups and forums online. LinkedIn groups, Reddit communities like r/netsec, and professional organizations like ISACA or the Information Systems Security Association (ISSA) are great places to start. All of these organizations have cybersecurity segments that offer a platform of both learning and sharing that you can take advantage of to build your brand.

Create a professional online presence. This can include a LinkedIn profile, a personal website, or a blog where you discuss cybersecurity topics, share projects, or write about your learning journey. People want to know what and how others are struggling and succeeding in their cybersecurity voyages. You can also contribute to open-source cybersecurity projects or publish your own. This showcases your skills and commitment to the field. The cybersecurity field is constantly evolving, so staying updated with the latest trends, threats, and technologies is crucial. Write about what you learn and share new experiences that surprised you. I can almost guarantee that others will find this interesting and start cross-referencing your work in social media. If you've decided to specialize in a particular area of cybersecurity, such as penetration testing, digital forensics, or security analysis, publishing blogs about your experiences can make you more attractive to employers in that niche.

Getting involved with mentorship programs is also a valuable way to create visibility for yourself. Seek mentorship from experienced professionals in the field via some of the nonprofits previously mentioned, for example, Cyversity, which has an excellent mentorship program. They can provide guidance, advice, and potentially even job leads. Eventually, you may find yourself mentoring less experienced people who find themselves on a similar path to the one you recently walked. Embrace this continuous bilateral learning and development. The field of cybersecurity is dynamic, and ongoing personal education is essential to stay relevant.

A number of interviewees recommended attending cybersecurity job/career fairs, even if you're not actively looking for a new job. They suggest that such forums are good places to have informal conversations with potential employees and employers, which is beneficial for those who prefer an outside-the-office informal interview setting. In addition to attending local trade shows, sign up to become a member of local risk and security groups, for example, ISACA, OWASP, and CSNP.

"The more you are out there in person and cyberspace, the more you'll get noticed" was the comment from a 20-year veteran in cybersecurity who values the proactive nature of a person as much as the capabilities. As one of my colleagues said, "My first security job was a referral from two people I was affiliated with via a nonprofit organization. On a related note, I hired someone I met at a local Boston ISACA event, and he's still with the company today."

Network

While your network naturally evolves as you get more involved in various cybersecurity communities, I view the word *network* more as a verb than a noun. You have to be constantly connecting, following up, and establishing relationships with key influencers, whether that be experts in specific topics, people at organizations that are hiring, or well-respected folks who can provide a reference for you. However, most people won't be willing to support you unless you put the effort into demonstrating passion, continued learning, and assertiveness (which should not be mistaken as being an extrovert; they are quite different). Networking boosts your chances of getting direct consideration for a role while you're focusing on building your skills.

A former co-worker of mine, Joe Basirico, who has long been a supporter of science, technology, engineering, and math (STEM) education, particularly in younger populations, wrote to me:

> "There are incredible resources available in security now. Great books, websites, tools, technologies, vulnerable practice websites, and apps. Use those to dive into security. Security is so vast that it's hard to find your place, but try things out until you find your passion, then dive deep. Ask questions. The people in security are amazing and helpful and love to teach others ... there's never been a better time to get into security than now."

Another very well-respected colleague, Kim Jones, said, "Your network is everything; develop it and use it. Get out there, be seen, donate time, do internships." Kim is a staunch advocate for hiring managers to get real with respect to what entry-level means and stop talking about a talent gap. In his words, "There is no cyber talent gap, but there is a cyber experience gap."

One young cybersecurity professional I had the pleasure of working with is also an active member of the cyber LGBTQ+ community, which, by the way, is a very small and disjointed one (but that's a topic for another day). He told me, "The only advice that I think is truly universal is *find a community*. The thing that pushed me forward, more than anything else, and the only thing that I think would be sort of non-negotiable for being in the industry is membership into some sort of group where conversation and sharing happens."

My friend, Mark Merkow, author of 18 books at my last count and long-time cybersecurity industry veteran says, "Networking is key. It's the first opportunity to determine if you really want to work with the kind of people who are in the industry. Exposure opens opportunities to learn and determine what areas of cybersecurity are most interesting to you, if any."

A recommendation I mentioned previously was echoed by a female CISO who found her path to cybersecurity leadership through communication and networking. She advises, "Find what interests you about the field and do your research. Talk to people. Do a self-inventory of your talents (the NICE cybersecurity training framework self-assessment is a great tool) and learn how they translate cybersecurity skills. If you have questions, ask someone. If you're shy, use email or user forums to get answers." This particular CISO loves security frameworks and standards. She and I even collaborated on a presentation we've delivered at several industry conferences. In that presentation, we offer a simple piece of advice to hiring managers and job seekers alike.

- Pick a cybersecurity standard, for example, PCI-DSS, and learn it (or even a section of it) very well.
- Take that knowledge and get networking help, for example, mentorship, that can provide advice on applying that knowledge practically in a job.
- Combine those pieces of knowledge into some impact statements you can use on resumes or job descriptions.

The result is an accurate, pragmatic, useful set of qualifications that can be matched to a job, whether it's on a jobs board or part of your internal human resources department.

Overcoming Challenges

When I created my initial research survey, I included this open-ended and optional question: "What's the biggest challenge you've had to

209

overcome in your cybersecurity career?" I did not expect so many people to offer answers to this question. These gracious souls also offered advice to those facing similar challenges. I did my best to refactor them into several categories. The categories are as follows:

- Organizational biases, silos, and disconnects
- Imposter syndrome and questioning competence
- Keeping skills up-to-date

There were several common challenges that individuals echoed but none as humorous to me as Edna Conway's biggest challenge: "Dealing with bloody acronym overload!"

Organizational Biases, Silos, and Disconnects

Organizational biases in cybersecurity can significantly impact the effectiveness of security strategies and confuse staff. These biases often stem from preconceived notions about threats, leading to a disproportionate focus on certain risks while neglecting others. For instance, there might be an overemphasis on external threats, over-looking the equally critical internal vulnerabilities. Such biases may arise from previous experiences, industry trends, or even media hype. One organizational bias is known as the *recency trap*, where companies overreact to a recent incident that occurred (internally or elsewhere) and over-invest time, attention, and money to deal with that while ignoring other higher-priority risk areas. To overcome this challenge, the value of threat modeling and risk management cannot be understated. These disciplines provide a measured framework for assessing risk. If a new threat emerges—for example, a company is made aware of a recent attack at a competitor—threat models can help them assess if that threat is an active, persistent, or serious threat to their organization.

Additionally, *confirmation bias* can cause security teams to favor information that supports their existing beliefs or strategies, potentially ignoring new or contradictory data. Addressing these biases is crucial for a comprehensive and adaptive cybersecurity approach, ensuring all potential risks are adequately assessed and mitigated.

Related to organizational structure, tensions, and the desire to view security teams as a reactive group, only to be heard from when there's a problem, several interviewees highlighted specific barriers to productivity. These are not necessarily actionable pieces of advice for job seekers; however, they are useful to anyone actively practicing or interacting with cybersecurity teams.

Stan Black's biggest challenge in his career has been "managing the gray spectrum of security." He cautions leaders to remember, "The question 'Are we secure?' does not have a yes or no answer." Stan has an interesting perspective because he has been both a practicing cybersecurity corporate executive and a consulting professional providing advice and solutions to his clients.

Several people cited the disconnect between various teams. Matthew Rosenquist and Florence Mottay, each with more than 20 years of cybersecurity experience, both said that security teams are often misunderstood or ignored. "The biggest challenge is that cybersecurity is often not relevant until it fails," said Matthew, while Florence said her biggest challenge is to "Get others to understand what I do!"

This is related to the silos that many organizations create, sometimes unwittingly, with respect to cybersecurity. This isolation often happens between builders/operators (yellow teams) and breakers/defenders (red and blue teams). Security teams bring vulnerabilities to the attention of the IT teams but find it challenging to translate that "what" into a "why" when asking IT teams to take some action to remove or mitigate those vulnerabilities. Similarly, many business and HR teams make the faulty assumption that cybersecurity is a purely technical field and nontechies have no place there. Charles Kolodgy, a

Straight from the Heart (of Cyber)

well-known cybersecurity industry analyst, says there is still a "disconnect between technical versus nontechnical positions. There seems to be an assumption that cybersecurity is a completely technical discipline. There are many nontechnical positions."

Many others cited the disconnects between nonsecurity executives with respect to security risks. "Bridging the gap with the business," "organizational politics," and "board of directors" were commonly identified as the biggest challenges my interviewees had to overcome in their careers. Closely related were things like "navigating embedded practices and power structures that are usually very resistant to change" and "geographical limitations on the types of industries that need cybersecurity professionals." This speaks to the importance of the research element when considering certain organizations or industries in which to pursue cybersecurity as a career.

Imposter Syndrome and Questioning Competency

One of the first lines I wrote for this book was "I am an imposter." Imposture syndrome in cybersecurity is very real indeed. Impostor syndrome in cybersecurity refers to the pervasive feeling of self-doubt and inadequacy experienced by professionals despite their qualifications and achievements. This phenomenon is particularly prevalent in our fast-paced, ever-evolving field of cybersecurity, where constant technological advancements and the critical nature of the work can intensify feelings of not being skilled or knowledgeable enough. Cybersecurity professionals, from beginners to experts, may feel like they're not truly deserving of their roles or accomplishments. This can lead to stress, burnout, and hindered performance. Admittedly, many of my research interviewees felt the same way. Addressing impostor syndrome involves acknowledging its presence, seeking support, and recognizing one's own expertise and contributions to the field.

Imposter syndrome in cybersecurity is largely driven by the thought that those in the field have to possess deeply technical skills and/or demonstrate their mastery of some system hack. This is not true. There is a lot more that goes into reducing risk and securing technology. In fact, in my experience, on the job is where people do most of their learning; therefore, the expectation should be that the candidate has the capability to learn, not that they know everything walking into any particular job. This is important for individuals and organizations alike to keep in mind. Set realistic requirements for jobs, knowing that 50–80 percent of practical skills will be learned in the first year on the job when working with others. This is why training and treating entry-level positions more as apprentices and less like experienced cybersecurity professionals is so important. Doing so allows staff to build confidence that they have the right makeup (not necessarily skills) straight out of the gate for the responsibilities they'll be asked to own in any given job.

Imposture syndrome is most commonly associated with an individual feeling that they don't belong. This is often related to that individual not having the perceived necessary level of education. One interview struck me as particularly poignant. This person is presently a CISO for a financial services company; however, prior to that he had an illustrious career in cybersecurity, including stints at more than one Fortune 100 company. Yet he still suffered from feeling as if he somehow didn't belong. Why? In his own words, "Lack of formal education. I went to a vocational high school where I learned to develop software in high school and skipped college." He felt that this lack of a degree was an invisible weight on his shoulders, a talisman that told others he wasn't qualified enough to be a cybersecurity practitioner. He told me, "Getting a formal education, training, and certification provides more options for getting started." It is a legitimate barrier for many people; however, look to this man's shining example of success in the face of that hurdle.

Imposter syndrome and questioning competency works in both directions. Some managers over- or under-estimate staff competencies, which leads them to make poorly informed decisions. This lack of group competency assessment is a major challenge to leaders and managers. Hiring managers may not even interview a candidate if they don't possess a four-year degree, despite the candidate having more than ample skills and experience. Conversely, a candidate with a bachelor's degree in computer science may be considered for a job they aren't actually qualified for, resulting in poor performance and increased risk to the hiring company. This is why diligent care must be given to crafting job descriptions.

Leaders in the field must be very mindful to be accurate with their requirements, must-haves, and nice-to-haves. Listing too many must-haves may prevent qualified candidates from applying. This is proven to be true for women and other minority demographics. One female CISO, who is also a person of color, told me that the single biggest challenge she had to overcome in her cybersecurity career was "Proving that my talents and skills matter and are needed in the field." That is a sad state of affairs because I know this woman and have worked with her; she is brilliant, passionate, motivated, articulate, and inspiring. She clearly defeated those biases and made a wonderful career for herself, achieving a C-level position before the age of 40.

Another young man, still in his early 20s when interviewed for this book, took a proactive approach. He is methodical about self-inventory and makes a practice of "Taking up my weakness as a challenge and making time to develop those weaknesses for the role I am in (or want to be in)."

Keeping Your Skills Up-to-Date

While many professions require current skills, the cybersecurity and technology fields are particularly fast-moving, making this a challenge.

New tech stacks, attacks, vulnerabilities, standards, and regulations appear each year. Regardless of how much security knowledge your job requires, a passion for continual learning is required in security. That said, be mindful to not fall into the imposter syndrome trap. One of my interviewees, who has enjoyed a very successful career in cybersecurity, advises, "You don't need to know it all; you just need to figure out the means to learn." This is echoed again and again by the professionals I interviewed.

Still, the advice of developing the capacity to learn is often colored with the paramount need to keep (at least some of) your skills modern. Consider the following five statements taken from my research interviews. They all identify this as a challenge; yet, a necessary one to remain relevant. Note how even for people who are now CIOs and CISOs, staying abreast of the latest and greatest developments for one's skill set is still a massive challenge. If you feel similarly about these challenges, you are not alone.

- "Keeping current on all the pertinent developments in the field" —from a CIO and former CISO

- "Staying on top of unrelenting technology change" —from a cybersecurity investment banker

- "Keeping up with the sheer pace of change in the tech landscape and being able to make sense of emerging threats" —from a CIO and long-time technology executive

- "For me, it's always been the pace. There is never enough time to understand all the different aspects as deeply as you would like to." —from a CISO and former IT security architect

- "Ongoing development/programming skills" —from an entry-level cybersecurity professional

What Hiring Managers Look For

This is a question I get asked all the time: "What do cybersecurity hiring managers *really* want in an entry-level candidate?" My perspective is myopic and biased, as it's a single point of view, so I asked 150 of my contacts a closely related question.

> "If you're involved in hiring for entry cybersecurity roles, what are the traits you're looking for beyond the résumé skills, education, and knowledge?"

Their answers were fascinating. I provided three choices and left a fourth field open-ended as "other." Respondents could choose more than one answer, yet only 28 percent felt the need to add something in the "other" field. The rest were happy to choose from the three options I provided.

By far, the most commonly selected answer, chosen by a whopping 90 percent of respondents, was "willingness to learn/be taught what they don't know." Although this may seem like a very encouraging answer to those seeking entry-level cybersecurity positions, some in the industry, my friend Kim Jones and I included, would say that this is not necessarily a completely earnest statement.

In his RSA Conference blogs from 2023 titled "Bridging the Talent Gap – Throwing the Gauntlet,"[1] Kim challenges cybersecurity hiring managers and HR departments to accept that "entry-level positions have a starting experience timeframe of zero." He further attests "there is no cyber talent gap. Rather, there's a cyber experience gap that we ourselves have created because we're too scared to take our

---

[1] www.rsaconference.com/Library/blog/bridging-the-talent-gap-part-1
www.rsaconference.com/Library/blog/bridging-the-talent-gap-part-2

eye off the tactical ball in order to edify and train a cadre of personnel to follow in our footsteps." Though 90 percent of hiring managers look for entry-level talent who is willing to learn/be taught what they don't know, many still seek some form of experience before offering an entry-level job to a candidate. This paradox is a hypocrisy that Kim Jones and others are trying to destroy via honest self-assessment.

Stepping aside from the entry-level qualification battle waging in the industry, let's take the survey responses at face value and dig a bit further into the answers. When hiring for entry cybersecurity roles, candidates who are open to learning is, undoubtedly, a treasured characteristic for managers. Even some respondents who chose "other" added a comment that speaks to this same trait. "A *learn it all* rather than a *know it all* approach" is one that stuck out to me. Another comment asked, "Do they learn in their spare time for fun?" Others still married the learning with an importance to seek mentorship: "Being inquisitive and willing to learn. Mentoring is also key. Find one you connect with and learn from them. Growing in the ranks of security requires an understanding of technology *and* business—your mentor should be able to guide you through that." Figure 8.5 shows these various answers in a chart.

Beyond the answers you can see in the histogram in Figure 8.5, I have (as I've done for other interview responses) refactored the qualitative answers into several similar categories.

- Curiosity and drive

- Demonstrated skill

- Attitude

Curiosity and Drive

An inherent curiosity and a self-driven desire to learn are vital for entry-level cybersecurity professionals. As discussed in the previous

217

section, this rapidly evolving field demands continuous learning to keep pace with emerging technologies and evolving threats. Curiosity fuels the exploration of new concepts, tools, and techniques, essential for staying ahead in cybersecurity. It drives professionals to question, investigate, and understand the intricate details of security systems and potential vulnerabilities. A self-driven approach to learning fosters adaptability and innovation, enabling professionals to proactively identify and address security challenges. This mindset not only accelerates personal growth but also contributes significantly to the resilience and advancement of cybersecurity practices in any organization.

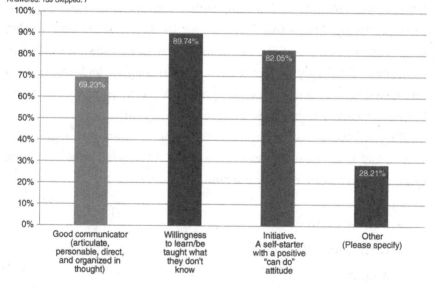

If you're involved in hiring for entry cybersecurity roles, what are the traits you're looking for beyond the resume skills, education, and knowledge?
Answered: 139 Skipped: 7

Figure 8.5 Answers to the question "What are the traits you are looking for beyond résumé skills, education, and knowledge?"

The manifestations of curiosity and drive presented themselves in the comments made by my interviewees. This list is a representative sample with corresponding attribution to help you qualify the "who?" with what was said:

- "Motivations primarily—critical thinking and adaptability too." This comment is from a friend of mine, Joshua Corman. Josh's formal education is a bachelor of arts in philosophy. He went on to be a chief technology officer, chief security officer, and chief strategist for CISA's COVID Task Force, and he is considered the father of software bill of materials (SBOM) in public policy. What does his big brain of cybersecurity look for? Motivation and critical thinking.

- "We find that those who hold a trait of undying curiosity to learn how things work are best suited for cyber risk." This was said by a former military veteran who became CTO and CEO of various cybersecurity companies.

- A cautionary comment for hiring managers: "I feel like looking for 'initiative' ends up choosing for extroverts, so be careful." The comment was from an active cybersecurity practitioner in the healthcare industry. This individual happens to have a lot of self-drive and initiative; he researched a pervasive healthcare communication protocol, found security flaws in it, and ultimately presented his research at DEFCON. But, his comment is relevant and worth careful consideration. We must not confuse self-drive and desire to learn with ambition or aggressiveness. Some people's ambition can appear like self-drive when it is, in fact, coupled with aggression. Nothing kills team morale faster than know-it-alls who are aggressive. They can disrupt development and derail programs they deem misaligned with personal ambitions and desires.

Demonstrated Skills

Many of the skills needed for security positions are similar to those that are sought with other roles: drive, willingness to learn, critical thinking, and so on. So, be sure to emphasize these "soft skills" on your résumé and in interviews. Hiring managers, again, should think outside the box for someone with solid skills that has a big upside that can be realized with some mentoring and training.

That being said, with cybersecurity being such a dynamic space, the nonsoft skills you need today might be very different than six months in the future. This is why core skills such as understanding cybersecurity fundamentals are essential. Simple concepts such as the concept of least privilege and the value of multifactor authentication serve as the bedrock for building other security skills. Once those are present, all of the technology, process, and domain-specific knowledge can be built on them.

Several cybersecurity executives, all of whom have led large teams distributed around the globe, offer these comments regarding the importance of demonstrable skills:

- "Hands-on experience is most important, if available, even if not directly related to the job responsibilities."

- "A strategic understanding (basic is fine) of the value and challenges of cybersecurity."

- "Basic understanding of risk and risk management is the first thing I look for in a security level 1 candidate."

Attitude

Julian Waits is a self-proclaimed cybersecurity entrepreneur who has held jobs as a network engineer, VP of sales and business development, president, CEO, and senior VP of strategic alliances. He is also one of the cofounders of Cyversity and a genuine joy to speak with. Incidentally, his university degrees are in music and performing arts. His commentary during my interview encapsulates his own personality, but also the many things he seeks when mentoring or recruiting aspiring cybersecurity professionals.

"I want a good communicator. Someone who is articulate, personable, direct, and organized in thought. Someone who is willing to be taught what they don't know, a self-starter with a positive 'can do' attitude .... Passion, passion, passion!"

Others look for more collaborative personality traits. Bryson Bort, another cybersecurity entrepreneur and military veteran, looks for empathy: "Someone willing to help co-workers since we need to work as a team. Also empathy for the users or technology; I feel too often we denigrate the folks we're supposed to be helping as an industry instead of understanding why they are where they are."

This type of team player and coachability were also mentioned by people such as Chad Holmes, a cybersecurity evangelist and former practitioner:

"No one can destroy progress like someone who is an asshole. That's not to say that everyone must be nice or have great social skills, but manipulative, self-focused, or otherwise destructive personalities will do more harm than good. This is particularly challenging in many technology fields, including cybersecurity, where higher rates of neurodivergence can be mistaken for being difficult. When hiring, you must always look for not only the skills and traits that an applicant has today, but also those that can be trained. If a person's intent, work ethic, and interests

221

align then unintentionally prickly behavior can often be coached away by good leaders."

Others pointed to the fact that our dynamic space needs dynamic people. Because cybersecurity often deals with highly sensitive information and data breaches, people with a strong moral compass were also identified as having a higher likelihood of success and a long career. Attitude and passion often go hand in hand, as several of my interviewees mentioned when they told me they look for an appreciation and understanding of security—someone who demonstrates a passion for an area of cybersecurity by having examples outside of work, where they have put personal time into their growth and understanding of their passion.

Before you move on to the personal case studies, I have to share a job opening that one of the executives I interviewed for this book was hiring for at the time of its writing (see Figure 8.6). She uses the cybersecurity color wheel to describe aspects of the job because she also uses the color wheel to define work roles. The use of colors in and of itself has become pervasive and descriptive enough in this organization that the terms can be used in job descriptions. It is such a wonderful development to see. The position is head of security operations and the person is to lead three cybersecurity teams: the red team, the blue team, and the yellow team!

About the job

As the Head of the Security Operations (SecOps) team, you will lead three teams of security experts (1) the Red Team, dedicated to performing assessments (penetration testing, red team exercises, etc.), (2) the Blue Team, focused on security monitoring and incident response, and (3) the Yellow Team, dedicated to building security components necessary for the blue and red team to be successful. You will be part of the information security management team and contribute to growing the function supporting the entire organization.

Figure 8.6 Head of security operations job description

Case Studies

Now that you know cybersecurity's dirty little secret (you don't have to be a hard-core hacker or have a technical degree to get a job and thrive in the field), this section profiles a few people who have successful careers in cybersecurity. Their backgrounds may surprise you, but I hope they also inspire you.

Security talent comes from all walks of life! Note that every one of these case studies are real and known to me personally. They are just a few of hundreds of such examples that exist in virtually every area of cybersecurity.

From Bakery to Badass

Like others you may have read about in this book, Liza Leshchenko earned a nontechnical undergraduate degree. Hers was in psychology and philosophy. She did some work in that field before settling into a role as a manager at a bakery handling operations and generating daily reports on sales and inventory. Not feeling completely fulfilled in the role and seeking a career with a higher financial upside, she decided to join a continuing education program. Continuing ed comes in many flavors; this one was an accelerated "intro to IT" type of program. During her continuing education activities, Liza discovered a real enjoyment and passion for writing code in C++ (not a particularly easy language to master, in my opinion), and she had a teaching assistant (TA) who became somewhat of a mentor for her.

That TA had his own full-time job working for a cybersecurity company, and he encouraged Liza to follow her newly discovered technical passion and explore the world of cyber. This intrigued Liza, because it allowed her to combine passions: a love for understanding how humans think and a love for technology.

Note the various ingredients that are being mixed together here—finding one's passion, identifying and working with a mentor, combining personal and professional interests, and exploring the field on one's own time. This amalgamation was the fuel that drove Liza to interview for a job in technical support. The company she interviewed with had an interesting product line that was being used to teach cybersecurity to software engineers in a gamified manner that let those engineers temporarily be an evil hacker and exploit a vulnerable software application. After a successful round of interviews, Liza was provided an opportunity to join that company and work with that product in that hacker game environment. She now had an interesting way to better understand the psychology of hacking, learn more about software security, and begin her IT career. She left the bakery behind and joined that cybersecurity company.

Liza's job is one that isn't on the cybersecurity color wheel. It's one of those tangential positions I talked about in Chapter 2. I am going to focus on a few more of those to help illustrate these two points:

- Each person's path into cybersecurity is unique and can start from virtually any origin.
- There are many good paying, satisfying work roles outside of the technical hacking world.

From Shakespeare to SolarWinds

This short case study is one that is also not on the cybersecurity color wheel. Ericka Chickowski is a storyteller. She graduated from the University of Washington with an English degree and has been a journalist for well-known media firms like the *Los Angeles Times* and the *Seattle Post-Intelligencer*. In the first five years of her professional career she got a job writing for a company called SC Media. SC Media was an early trailblazer in covering the cybersecurity industry. That job gave Ericka the taste for cyber, and she was hooked. Over her illustrious career, she has written about the intersections of information technology, cybersecurity, enterprise risk, DevOps, and digital transformation. She has won numerous industry awards, cofounded Digirupt.io, and is a frequently cited expert of investigative cybersecurity reporting.

Ericka astutely surmised that the IT and cybersecurity fields would be exploding with innovation, risks, and world-changing stories throughout the 2010s and 2020s. Not only was she right about that, but she has been at the forefront of writing about it with an audience of tens of millions who read her articles on a regular basis. Ericka has established herself as a subject-matter expert in our industry. In fact, when I wanted to create a show for Ed TALKS (`www.edtalks.io`) about "Movers & Shakers in DevSecOps," I asked Ericka to be one of my guests, along with Shannon Lietz, the founder of the DevSecOps Foundation, and Mark Merkow, the author of 18 books on software security. This is the type of company that this English graduate now runs, all driven by her own passion to take her talents and apply them in her own unique way to an industry exploding with information and intrigue. The result has been an extraordinary career.

From Pharmacy to Phishing

Damon DePaolo's job is on the cybersecurity color wheel. He is part of that guiding light of white discussed in Chapter 5. He is presently the director of cybersecurity talent and education at a Fortune 100 company. But he certainly didn't start there. Damon did go to college, but his was more of a business and information management focus, and he chose to take time off after his first two years. He took a job with a drugstore chain that he had worked at while he was going to university. After being promoted to assistant store manager and serving in that capacity for a couple of years, Damon decided to try a job that was more information-focused and less business-focused. It was a stretch for him, but he had taught himself some basic programming skills using visual programming languages, and he wanted to do something in that field. He got a job as a systems consultant, where he performed systems analysis and assisted with business process improvement (BPI) projects. This was his launching pad.

Those BPI projects with an information systems bent led him to be a lead spokesperson for what we now call *digital transformation*. He started to write and speak about the importance of human-centered design during BPI, and that inevitably led him to cybersecurity. Combining the personal skills inventory he built during his career, he decided it was time to earn that college degree. First, he finished an associate degree in information systems and then later a bachelor's degree in information systems. By the time he had earned his bachelor degree, he had also cultivated an interest in cybersecurity's human elements. That led him to inquire about the security education program at his large employer. His initiative paid off, and he was offered a job in that very group. A steady line of promotions followed, and he now is at that director role previously mentioned. Initiative, self-inventory, and assertiveness all played integral parts in Damon's ascent in cybersecurity.

From Sales and Marketing to Cyber SMEs

I interviewed several people in the sales and marketing domains for this book; however, I also know quite a few more sales and marketing professionals who work for security companies and have made exceptional careers out of it. I briefly discuss two such people who I had the honor of working with directly over the past decade.

Both of them earned a bachelor's degree, but neither was in a technical discipline—one was in business, the other liberal arts.

The liberal arts major started his career in the hospitality and entertainment industry, dealing cards at casinos and bartending. The business major began her career as a marketing associate for a solar energy company.

Each one of them decided they wanted to broaden their horizons and earn more money, so they looked to the technology sector for their next jobs. They both got into the IT software industry around the same time in the late 1990s. Although they took separate paths, each realized they had a strong capacity for understanding the technical sides of the product and services they were marketing and selling, respectively. The sales professional got into the world of software testing and quality assurance; the marketing pro found herself representing products aimed at IT administrators. Both were pitching their wares to yellow teams; both parlayed that experience into the world of securing IT systems and software, which as you've learned in this book, is a logical extension for yellow teams.

The sales guy leveraged his experience selling software testing solutions to land a job with a company who was delivering penetration testing services to large software vendors such as Microsoft, Symantec, and Amazon. A couple of years prior, the marketing woman got a job at that same company. She created positioning documents, rebuilt the company website, and helped create thought leadership pieces to establish the firm as a go-to source for software penetration testing. These two found each other in cybersecurity though they came from disparate paths. Through their respective work, they listened, learned, and asked many questions of the engineers and leaders at that organization. This helped them build their own credibility and subject-matter expertise. In fact, the two became so well informed about software security that the marketing woman took on the job of writing technical blogs, creating webinar content, and even crafting the bios of billable penetration test engineers at

227

the company that the sales guy would then use to sell the company's expert services.

The sales rep got to the point where he could take a sales opportunity very far before needing to engage any technical assistance. He could now write his own sales proposals, including much of the technical language, to better address specific needs of clients. He regularly engaged in trusted advisor relationships without having to always rely on technical engineers to assist. Both the sales and marketing professionals in this example also built on their particular backgrounds, added cybersecurity knowledge, and, through their own initiative, curiosity, and drive, established themselves as subject-matter experts for their respective teams.

They became security champions to other sales and marketing professionals at the company. They added value to themselves as employees and to their employer because they helped accelerate and disseminate security knowledge throughout teams not represented on the cybersecurity color wheel. This value-add is echoed in the following case study as well, but it manifests in two completely different groups.

Value-Added Cybersecurity Knowledge

Two recent examples I had the joy of experiencing firsthand include a cloud architect in Ireland and a director of support and implementation in the United States.

The cloud architect was listening to a presentation on cybersecurity—my presentation. I was walking through the various colors and discussing how security can be a value-add to jobs in the yellow team area. The cloud architect offered to the audience how the discussion helped cauterize for him the value of learning even just one simple thing about security, in this instance one of the

---

techniques in the MITRE ATT&CK Framework. His job, he said, was to take business requirements for a particular IT system that was to be built or updated and design the appropriate cloud servers, services, APIs, and communication protocols to meet the requirements.

He said that after hearing me use an example of a MITRE ATT&CK technique, he realized that a recent project needed to be changed. Even more heartwarming is that he said to the audience, "If I had been educated enough to know that this attack was possible, I would have gone back to that business owner and challenged him to modify one of the requirements because the use case they developed hadn't considered this particular abuse." He went on to say that the solution that incorporated the security safeguard was no more or less complicated than the one he had previously designed, meaning he would have been able to add value to his business and mitigate a potential threat without adding any cost or time to the IT solution.

The U.S.-based support and implementation director was having an exchange with the IT director at the same company. The IT director was planning to upgrade the firm to a different version of a collaboration SaaS platform and had notified his peers. The support director asked him if he could ensure that other users at the firm would not be able to see his collaboration "boards" unless they were explicitly authorized to do so, because the boards were being used to house sensitive client data that should not be visible to anyone outside of his direct functional group (support and implementation).

The IT director's response was something to the effect of "Yes, of course, that is a key feature of this particular upgrade. We'll now be able to enable permissions per workspace and allow for automation of role-based access controls via SAML connections." This exchange was music to my heart. Here is a yellow team member (IT director) and someone not even on the cybersecurity color wheel (tech support) having a meaningful conversation about security, segregation, and permission controls.

These two individuals collectively and individually increased the cybersecurity hygiene of their company. Having cyber-aware people like this heading up their groups is very valuable indeed. Most support leads wouldn't necessarily think of the confidentiality implications to customer data related to changes IT planned to internal collaboration software. Proactively surfacing these concerns because he was security-aware is a real value-add. And that IT director, likewise, had already factored that consideration (and other security concerns) into the requirements of that change.

If other noncybersecurity leaders want to up their personal value and add to the cybersecurity of their firm, they can do so by getting smarter about security, just as these two people did. It's good for the individual, it's good for the company, and it's good for the industry as a whole.

Summary

The final chapter of this book provided both empirical and anecdotal perspectives into cybersecurity careers. The comprehensive analysis of survey responses, coupled with my conversations with industry professionals, is intended to provide a well-rounded view of the many angles in which you can achieve success in cyber. I distilled a wealth of information from various cybersecurity professionals into a cohesive summary, highlighting the diverse and atypical paths to cybersecurity careers, with some real case studies to help cement the messages.

The two major sections of this chapter are meant to be companions to each other. The key findings were subdivided into categories such as getting into the cybersecurity industry, advice from practitioners, overcoming common challenges, and what hiring managers look for. The case studies provided representations of cyber journeys across various career paths that are both real and directly illustrative of the discussion topics regarding the cybersecurity color wheel "slices" in previous chapters.

I'd like to emphasize one final time: there is no typical path to a career in cybersecurity. I hope I've debunked some common myths and stereotypes. The cybersecurity industry has evolved from a predominantly technical field to one that encompasses and needs a broader range of talents, including business, legal, and communication skills. My own atypical journey into cybersecurity is but one of many that highlights the importance of diverse skills and continuous learning.

Survey insights reveal various paths to cybersecurity jobs, with more than 80 percent of professionals having had a mentor and the significance of networking. Even though many enter the field "by accident," an openness to new experiences is common among those in cybersecurity, as is the involvement of others to enable and transform individuals into cyber contributors.

For individuals unsure of where to start in cybersecurity, I suggest internships, entry-level positions, and joining relevant organizations. The chapter detailed various entry-level job roles, both technical and business-centric, and emphasized the importance of relevant certifications and continuous education.

The advice in this chapter provided by cybersecurity practitioners emphasized joining organizations, obtaining certifications, and finding one's passion. Practical experience was highlighted as crucial, with suggestions including setting up lab environments, participating in online competitions, and volunteering.

I also discussed overcoming challenges in cybersecurity, such as organizational biases, imposter syndrome, and the need to keep skills up-to-date. Finally, the chapter delved into what hiring managers look for in candidates, emphasizing the willingness to learn and the paradox in hiring practices where entry-level positions often require experience.

Regardless of which color slice you prefer, every role in cybersecurity will have a primary focus on people, processes, or technology. Understanding which of these is your particular preference will help you find your way more quickly. Organizations that highlight the importance of security awareness across every job function in an enterprise will benefit by potentially heightening the impact of various work roles on organizational security culture and hygiene.

I talked at length about people who got into cybersecurity with backgrounds that started in the military, finance, marketing, legal, business, retail management, writing, and other nontechnical fields. The examples are seemingly endless. The opportunities and challenges in the industry are a focal point of the entire book; however, I have endeavored to provide some practical, actionable tips to help bridge the gap between talent and experience in the cybersecurity industry. I hope you have found this book, the related research, and the insights presented useful to your career or your current job.

About the Author

Ed Adams is a leader in the IT security and software quality industries. He is currently CEO of Security Innovation, has run global divisions of publicly traded corporations, and has held senior management positions at Rational Software, Lionbridge, and MathSoft.

He is a lifelong technology enthusiast whose love of engineering and liberal arts helped him forge a career in cybersecurity. Ed is passionate about advancing the cybersecurity workforce and education. He proudly serves Cyversity, a nonprofit organization that promotes diversity and inclusion in the field. He is a Privacy by Design ambassador for Canada and represents the Ponemon Institute as a Distinguished Research Fellow. No stranger to the podium, Ed has presented at numerous industry conferences and hosts Ed TALKS, an online talk show where he interviews cybersecurity experts on best practices and emerging trends.

Ed earned degrees in mechanical engineering and English Literature at the University of Massachusetts prior to receiving an MBA with honors from Boston College. He lives in Massachusetts with his wife and best friend, Maureen, and both are proud "Bay Staters." They enjoy traveling the world together and are fitness fiends; however, most of all, they love spending time with their large, extended family and friends.

Index

cybersecurity attorney, 196
cybersecurity audit, 107, 108–109
cybersecurity communications
    manager, 198
cybersecurity data analyst/scientist, 198
cybersecurity education and training
    manager, 195
cybersecurity engineer, 69
cybersecurity governance, as a respon-
    sibility of CISO, 105
cybersecurity hardware engineer, 17
cybersecurity insurance, 107–108
cybersecurity knowledge, needed for
    jobs not on color wheel, 26
cybersecurity law, 107
cybersecurity lawyer, 17, 102
Cybersecurity Magazine, 16
cybersecurity policies and proce-
    dures, as a responsibility
    of CISO, 105
cybersecurity practitioners, advice
    from, 199–209
cybersecurity Scrum master,
    17, 102, 109
cybersecurity software developer/
    engineer, 18
Cyversity, 144, 145, 161, 206–207,
    220–221

D

data in motion, 90
data loss prevention (DLP), 127
data privacy officer, 18, 102
data protection, cloud security
    and, 126–127
data recovery specialist, 18, 102
data security analyst, 18
database administrators (OM), 58
defenders, 14–15, 46
defense in depth, 39, 90

defense strategies, adaptive, as a value
    from purple teaming, 67
Definition stage, 51
Deloitte research, 137
demonstrated skills, hiring managers
    looking for, 220
denial-of-service (DoS) attack, 79–80, 90
DePaolo, Damon, 225–226
deploy/adopt phase
    in green teaming, 94–96
    in orange teaming, 85–86
Deployment and maintenance stage, 52
Design stage, 51
design/code phase
    in green teaming, 90–91
    in orange teaming, 81–82
developers, 52
DevOps, 52
digital forensics, 199
digital forensics analyst, 18
digital marketing manager, 23
digital transformation, 226
disaster recovery specialist, 18
disconnects, 210–211
diverse career paths, as a challenge for
    cybersecurity jobs, 26
diversity and inclusion (D&I)
    about, 135–136, 166–168
    achieving in U.S. cybersecurity
      industry, 146–151
    age gap, 147
    aligning expectations, 147–148
    benefits of, 136–138
    building programs for, 165–166
    case studies, 154–165
    as a challenge for cybersecurity
      jobs, 27
    in cybersecurity, 136–139
    drawbacks and dangers of, 138–139
    encouraging educational path-
      ways, 152–154
    increasing retention rate, 148–149